TIME
HEROES

*A Celebration of Hibernian's Glorious
2016 Scottish Cup Victory*

Ted Brack

BLACK & WHITE PUBLISHING

First published 2016
by Black & White Publishing Ltd
29 Ocean Drive, Edinburgh EH6 6JL

Reprinted 2016

3 5 7 9 10 8 6 4 2   16 17 18 19

ISBN: 978 1 78530 078 3

A CIP catalogue record for this book is available from the British Library.

Typeset by Iolaire, Newtonmore
Printed and bound by CPI Group (UK) Ltd, Croydon, CR0 4YY

MIX
Paper from
responsible sources
FSC
www.fsc.org   FSC® C013604

TIME FOR HEROES

Ted Brack

Ted Brock

This book is dedicated to my father-in-law Arthur Delaney and his sons Terry and Michael. They loved the Hibs and, in the company of 'the angels up above', they would have been celebrating with the rest of us on Saturday 21 May. God bless them.

Contents

Acknowledgements

In my first book, *There is a Bonny Fitba Team*, I wrote the following sentence in the Acknowledgements section: 'I promise you that if Hibs do eventually win the Scottish Cup, I will begin writing the story of how they did it the very next day.' As we now know, at around 4.50pm on Saturday 21 May 2016 the ultimate Hibernian dream did indeed become reality.

I have a confession to make. I didn't start writing this book until two days after Hibs went up to lift the Scottish Cup. The Sunday after the final was of course the day of the victory parade and there was absolutely no possibility of any writing being done on that magical day. Forty-eight hours after the end of 114 years of hurt, I was seated at my laptop enjoying the experience of recording Hibernian history.

My task was made easier because all through season 2015–16, I had faithfully kept a journal of Hibs' progress. I had just harboured a feeling that 2016 might be Hibs year to finally capture the 'Scottish'. That feeling grew when the Hibees pulled back a two-goal deficit in the last ten minutes at Tynecastle in February. It strengthened further after the Conrad Logan show against Dundee United at Hampden in April and, of course, came to fruition on a momentous day in May.

Writing this book has been an absolute pleasure. A number of people have greatly helped me in doing so.

As always, I need to thank my wife Margaret and my children Patrick, Lisa, Dominic and Kevin. They offered help and support in equal measure and both were greatly appreciated. Lisa's proof reading was meticulous and the family's suggestions for enhancing the book made a definite difference.

May I also thank one of my former pupils Charlotte Lauder. Charlotte is now an undergraduate and a historian in the making. At school, Charlotte was intelligent, conscientious and highly organised. She brought all of these qualities to bear in carrying out invaluable research on my behalf into Hibs ten losing Scottish Cup finals from 1914 to 2013.

Thanks are due too to Campbell Brown and everyone at Black & White Publishing for ensuring that this book was in the shops while the warm glow of success continued to linger in every Hibernian heart. Campbell has always shown faith in my work and I greatly appreciate the backing and assistance that he has given me.

A sincere thank you to everyone who buys this book. I hope you obtain as much pleasure from reading it as I did from writing it.

Finally a massive vote of thanks to Alan Stubbs, his staff, the club board which backed them and the players who wore the famous green and white on that day of all days at Hampden for finally bringing home the Holy Grail.

Foreword

by DAVID GRAY
Captain, Hibernian FC

Hibs suffered two major disappointments last season. We lost a League Cup final to Ross County that we felt we should have won and we missed out on promotion back to the Premiership when Falkirk scored in added-on time to beat us in the second leg of the play-off semi-final. Both legs of the play-off could easily have gone our way so losing out so late on in the tie was very hard for us to take.

As captain, I felt that I had to use these setbacks as motivation for our Scottish Cup final against Rangers. My message to my teammates was that we still had a great chance to make season 2015–16 special and that we should make sure that we didn't miss out on that opportunity.

As the cup final went on and, despite playing well, we were trailing 2–1, I realised that we would have to start taking a few more risks to get back into it. Once we equalised, I really felt that we were going to do it.

Liam Fontaine and I had been talking in our hotel room on the night before the game about the dream scenario of Hibs scoring a stoppage-time winner against Rangers. Little did I imagine that it would actually happen and that I would be the person to make history.

When my header bulleted into the net, all sorts of thoughts were going through my mind. I just remember being amongst the crowd celebrating and the referee telling me that he was sorry but he would have to apply the rules and book me. Believe you me, I wasn't complaining!

It was great to help Hibs win the Scottish Cup at last for our tremendous fans, who have stuck with us through thick and thin. No one has waited longer than 106-year-old Sam Martinez so it was good to have a drink for him on the Saturday night.

The scenes when we brought the Scottish Cup through Leith and down to the Links on the Sunday were truly amazing and will live long in the memories of all of us. The only thing that stopped our season from being perfect was the fact that we didn't manage to win promotion. That will be our prime target for season 2016–17 and capturing the Scottish Cup has given us the belief that we can do exactly that.

It is great that our achievement is already being recognised in a book and I wish Ted every success with *Time for Heroes*.

David Gray

Introduction

At around 4.50pm on Saturday 18 April 2015, I trudged out of Scotland's national stadium at Hampden in a state of abject depression. I had just watched Hibernian – the football team I have loved all my life – lose 1–0 to Falkirk in the Scottish Cup semi-final.

Hibs had played well and dominated the game but Falkirk had survived defensively and Craig Sibbald had clinically headed home the one meaningful chance that the Bairns had created. As I left the ground, I was convinced that, approaching my 68th birthday, I would not live long enough to see laid to rest a Scottish Cup hoodoo which at that point amounted to a scarcely credible 113 years without Hibs ever lifting the oldest trophy in world football.

That season ended and Hibs narrowly missed promotion to the Scottish Premiership in which they belong. During the summer, a strange thing happened. I began to have a sense that season 2015–16 was going to be a special one for my club. I decided to keep a journal of the season. As each month progressed, I faithfully recorded the ups and downs of a season that turned out to be a total rollercoaster ride.

When Hibs went up to lift the Scottish Cup on 21 May 2016, as the song says, I was there. My wildest dream had been realised and what for so long had seemed impossible had become reality. I was so glad that I had kept a month-by-month record of the most memorable of seasons.

This book went to the printers within two weeks of Hibs Scottish Cup win just as John McGinn was receiving a richly merited Championship Player of the Year Award. I wanted to share my story of glory with the Hibs support while the warm glow of victory still remained. We know that Neil Lennon has succeeded Alan Stubbs as Hibs manager and, by the time this journal reaches the bookshops, we will also have learned what action the SFA has decided to take against Hibs for the pitch invasion that followed referee Steven McLean's final whistle at the end of the Scottish Cup final.

These are important matters but they are not the subject matter of this book. This is a record of a Hibernian season which fluctuated between highs and lows, but which ended on the most positive possible note as David Gray mounted the steps up to the presentation area of the main stand at Hampden to receive and hold aloft the Scottish Cup after 114 years of hurt. What a moment. What a season. I am hugely honoured to be able to tell the story of Hibs' long-awaited Scottish Cup triumph.

Ted Brack, June 2016

PROLOGUE

The Agony: Relegation and Rehabilitation

In the final match of season 2013–14, Hibernian Football Club delivered an abject performance at home to Hamilton Academicals in the second leg of the Premiership Play-Off Final and in the process threw away the two-goal lead they had earned in the first leg at New Douglas Park. The result was relegation to the Scottish Championship.

A team with a deeply loyal support, a state-of-the-art training centre and a magnificent modern stadium had reached a nadir in its fortunes. It was not difficult to see why this had happened. A succession of poor managerial appointments had led to the signing of journeymen players and the performance of these players had led to demotion. As successive managers were relieved of their duties and received financial settlements and players of poor standards were released early from their contracts and received pay-offs, Hibs – a club renowned for its fiscal prudence – wasted money that could have been put to much better use.

At the end of the Hamilton match, television pictures showed me consoling my grandson Daniel who was crying his eyes out with disappointment. In truth, many older Hibs fans felt like weeping that day as well.

A summer of turbulence followed. Paul Kane – a lifelong Hibs supporter and an excellent player who served the club with distinction – organised a 'Petrie Out' campaign in a bid to oust the club chairman Rod Petrie. A rally in the car park of the West Stand at Easter Road attracted around 2,000 people. Pat Stanton, Jackie McNamara, Mickey Weir and Kenny McLean Junior (son of the late, great Kenny McLean who spearheaded the Hands Off Hibs campaign which thwarted Wallace Mercer's hostile bid to gain control of Hibs) all spoke of the need for change. Rebellion was most definitely in the air.

As the weeks went by, other protest groups sprung up. There were Hands On Hibs, Buy Hibs and Hibernian Forever. There was also an attempt to buy the club by a consortium whose public face was the football finance expert David Low.

Rod Petrie rode out the storm and remained chairman. He welcomed a new Chief Executive in Leeann Dempster, who joined Hibs after being extremely successful with Motherwell. Dempster walked into the proverbial baptism of fire but held her nerve and quickly made a positive impression.

She was accessible to supporters, spoke well and wasn't slow to take action. The manager Terry Butcher was sacked after less than a year in post. Butcher had been Hibs' eighth manager in ten years. A total of eighteen players were ultimately released. A new manager, Alan Stubbs, was appointed and he took up his post at a time when Hibs had a skeleton playing staff and a disaffected fan base.

The club was the subject of criticism in the media. BBC pundit Tom English described Hibs football under Butcher as 'prehistoric' and Sportscene regular Michael Stewart called it 'archaic'.

There was ridicule in everyday life. In the early summer, I visited Marks & Spencer's foreign exchange bureau to buy dollars. When I took out my wallet, which bore the Hibs crest and was well used to say the least, the cashier remarked, 'Your wallet is falling apart just like your team.' That was typical of the time.

To say that Stubbs had inherited a challenging situation would be the ultimate in understatements. He was an impressive figure though. This was a man with a great playing career behind him, coaching experience at his home city club Everton and the courage to survive two major cancer operations, the second of which had lasted for eight hours. This was not a man who would be easily fazed.

He struck the right note at the outset when he said that he wanted to give Hibs supporters a spring in their step again. That was something that had been missing for quite some time. Former Hibs striker Derek Riordan echoed Stubbs' words when he said Hibs had to start 'playing with swagger' again. He was absolutely right.

Leeann Dempster announced a plan for the club with a continental model in the management structure. Stubbs as Head Coach was at the top of the pyramid and he was joined in his coaching team by John Doolan and Andy Holden. George Craig came in as Head of Football Operations, Graeme Mathie as Head of Recruitment, Joe McBride as Development Squad Coach and Eddie May returned to Hibs as Head of Youth Development.

Things moved forward on the playing side too. Stubbs' first signing was right-back David Gray from Burton Albion and what a significant acquisition that was to prove. Gray was joined by Farid El Alagui, Scott Allan, Mark Oxley, Liam Fontaine, Dylan McGeouch and Dominique Malonga. In stark contrast to the flawed recruitment policies of his predecessors, Alan Stubbs had brought quality players to Hibs.

The 2014–15 league campaign was going to be difficult as Hibs had to compete with both Hearts and Rangers as they attempted to win promotion at the first time of asking. Things didn't start well and three of the first four games were lost. However, at Ibrox in September, Hibs won 3–1 and the precociously talented Jason Cummings, scorer of two of the goals, announced insouciantly that he had 'the touch of an angel'. Hibs other goal was scored by David Gray who would make a habit of being on the target against the Light Blues.

As the season progressed, the team began to play with style but didn't always convert that superiority into results. Scott Allan emerged as Hibs' best midfield playmaker since Russell Latapy and there were encouraging performances in derby matches.

An attempt had been made earlier in the season to bring Leigh Griffiths to Easter Road from Celtic on loan. Griffiths inexplicably had not been in new Celtic manager Ronny Deila's plans. The move didn't materialise, though, and when Deila eventually gave Griffiths a first-team opportunity in November, he rewarded him by keeping his place and scoring twenty goals by the end of the season. If Hibs had captured Griffiths – and they very nearly did – their season would have been transformed.

As it was, goal scoring proved difficult. Cummings was frequently on target but missed his fair share of chances too. Malonga chipped in regularly as well but the loss of El Alagui to a long-term injury too often meant that when the main strikers didn't score, Hibs didn't have many other scoring options and this led to the unnecessary loss of important points.

2014 ended well though. Hibs beat Rangers 4–0 at Easter Road. It was as convincing and impressive a performance as Hibs fans had seen for a long time and they greeted it rapturously.

There was good news off the field too. Hibs announced that agreement had been reached with the club owner Sir Tom Farmer and the Bank of Scotland to clear all bank debt and reduce and restructure the remaining debt. There would also be a share issue and the potential for fans to own 51% of the club if enough of them came forward to invest. People like Pat Stanton, Jackie McNamara and Charlie Reid of the Proclaimers, who had previously opposed the direction in which the club was moving were happy to back this proposal. The earlier unrest was becoming a thing of the past and harmony was returning to Easter Road.

As the Championship campaign moved towards its conclusion, it became clear that Hearts were going to win the league and the automatic promotion which went with it. They had been consistent all season. While Hibs, so much more attractive under Stubbs, had perfected the art of dominating games but often only managing to draw them and sometimes even losing them, Hearts were adept at staying in games and grinding out results even when their performance wasn't all that impressive.

Hibs beat Rangers again at Ibrox in February and convincingly won the last derby of the season at Easter Road. Falkirk, who were proving resilient and ultra-competitive under Peter Houston, were defeated in the last league game and Hibs finished the season in second place – a commendable achievement on the part of Alan Stubbs given the shambles which he had inherited when he had come to Hibs.

Rangers and Hibs contested the play-off semi-finals. Rangers took their chances in the first leg at Ibrox while Hibs missed theirs. The resultant 2–0 home victory gave Hibs a mountain to climb in the return leg at Easter Road. In front of a packed ground, they very nearly did climb that mountain. They bombarded Rangers and could have scored four or five goals. In the end, they had a solitary Jason Cummings counter to show for their efforts.

At full time, in complete contrast to the end of the final match of the previous season, the crowd stood to applaud Hibs warmly. They knew that this had been a season of improvement. Scott Allan, who had pulled the midfield strings with increasing authority as the season unfolded, was voted Scottish Championship Player of the Year. Alan Stubbs was attracting attention from English clubs, which had to mean that he was doing a really good job and the feel-good factor was back.

Rangers expended so much energy in managing to scrape through against Hibs that they had little left in their tank when the Play-Off Final came round and they lost tamely to Motherwell, thus ensuring that they would be competing with Hibs again in the Championship in 2015–16.

Alan Stubbs didn't just do well in the league though. He also made progress in the cup competitions. Hibs made the quarter-finals of the League Cup and lost to Dundee United, who at that time were doing well only after extra time and penalties.

In the Scottish Cup, Hibs saw off Alloa, Arbroath and Berwick Rangers to reach the semi-finals. There they met Peter Houston's Falkirk. Falkirk got ten men behind the ball, survived due to a combination of resolute defending, profligate Hibs finishing and good fortune and managed to score with their only attack of note in the match. Alan Stubbs said after Hibs' 1–0 defeat that Falkirk had been lucky. Peter Houston countered by claiming that Hibs couldn't defend cross balls. There was truth in both managers' statements.

As I left Hampden in a state of deep depression that day, I genuinely felt that I wasn't going to live to see Hibs capture the Scottish Cup. Since last winning it in 1902, Hibs had managed to lose ten finals and numerous semi-finals. It was as though they were cursed in the competition and their extended failure to capture Scotland's premier knockout trophy was a source of embarrassment to all Hibs supporters as well as an excuse for fans of other clubs to mock the Hibees, which they did with great regularity.

How a club of Hibs' stature could have gone so long without winning a tournament that requires only five ties to be negotiated before success is achieved was a matter of mystery. It wasn't as if the club hadn't had its opportunities since last winning the 'Scottish' in 1902.

When the then Hibs' manager Dan McMichael and his team of Harry Rennie, Archie Gray, Bobby Glen, Barney Breslin, Jimmy Harrower, Alex Robertson, Johnny McCall, Andy McGeachan, Johnny Divers, Paddy Callaghan and Bobby Atherton paraded the Scottish Cup along Princes Street on a horse-drawn break led by the Newhaven Brass Band playing 'See the Conquering Hero Comes', they could never have dreamt just how long it would take for another Hibs team to emulate their success. At the time, Philip Farmer – one of the club's directors and a relative of current majority shareholder Sir Tom Farmer – declared himself 'the proudest man in Great Britain' and said 'Hibernian have attained their heart's desire'. Over a century would pass before that coveted prize would be captured again and by then it had turned into a Holy Grail for all Hibs fans.

In 1914, three months before the outbreak of the First World War, Hibs travelled to Ibrox to do battle with Celtic in the Scottish Cup Final. Dan McMichael was again the manager and his team was Willie Allan, Neil Girdwood, Bobby Templeton, Peter Kerr, Matta Paterson, Sandy Grossert, Bobby Wilson, Sam Fleming, Jimmy Hendren, Jock Wood and Willie Smith.

Paterson, the imperious captain, was known as 'the Czar' and the goalkeeper Allan went by the nickname of 'Masterman Ready'. Chicago born right-winger Wilson's goals had helped Hibs reach the final but when the game was played, neither team was able to score. In their early years, Hibs never had life made easy by the Scottish footballing authorities and this occasion was to prove no different. The replay was set for the Thursday after the original match and Hibs were made to play a league game the day before it. It is hardly surprising then that a very tired Hibs team lost the cup final replay 4–1 with their goal coming from left-winger Willie Smith who was known as 'the uncrowned King of Easter Road'.

Hibs were in the final again in 1923 and once more Celtic were their opponents. This time the match was played at Hampden. The BBC had just been granted a licence to broadcast but I don't think they covered the final! Howard Carter unsealed the tomb of Tutankhamun in this year but there was to be no gleaming silverware for Hibs at Hampden. Hibs team of Willie Harper, Willie McGinnigle, Willie Dornan, Peter Kerr, Willie Miller, Hugh Shaw, Harry Ritchie, Jimmy Dunn, Jimmy McColl, Johnny Halligan and John Walker lost 1–0. Ironically the goal resulted from an error by the normally outstanding goalkeeper Harper. The forward line of Ritchie, Dunn, McColl, Halligan and Walker was Hibs' first great front five. McColl had scored twice against Hibs in the 1914 final but he was unable to get on the score sheet against his old club. The diminutive, ginger-headed 'Tim' Dunn went on to become a member of the 1928 Scotland Wembley Wizards team which beat England 5–1 at Wembley. Hibs were managed by Alex Maley and Celtic were under the control of his brother Willie.

A year later Hibs were once again in the final of the Scottish Cup. Their opponents were Airdrieonians and the match was played at Ibrox. Hibs lost 2–0 to what was Airdrie's greatest ever side featuring such luminaries as Hughie Gallagher and Bob McPhail. Hibs fielded the same eleven as the previous season. These players were now known as 'The Celebrated Team' and of course that team included Hugh Shaw who would manage Hibs to great success in the 1940s and 50s. Gleneagles Hotel had opened its doors in 1924 but the doors of the Easter Road trophy cabinet remained firmly closed to the Scottish Cup.

When Hibs returned to Hampden for their first Scottish Cup Final in twenty-three years in the spring of 1947 after enduring one of the severest winters in Britain's history in the early part of the year, forty-five years and two world wars had gone by since they had last lifted the trophy. The team that set out to break what was now becoming a hoodoo was Jimmy Kerr, Jock Govan, Davie Shaw, Hugh Howie, Peter Aird, Sammy Kean, Gordon Smith, Willie Finnigan, Johnny Cuthbertson, Eddie Turnbull and Willie Ormond. Not even the presence of three members of the Famous Five (the teenaged Lawrie Reilly just missed out on selection) could help Hibs lift that increasingly elusive trophy.

Hibs got off to a perfect start when Johnny Cuthbertson gave them the lead with only twenty-five seconds on the clock and Jimmy Kerr saved an Aberdeen penalty. The Dons, though, still managed to run out 2–1 winners.

The period without Scottish Cup glory had stretched to fifty-six years when Hibs returned to the national stadium to meet Clyde in the 1958 final. February of that year had seen

Matt Busby's great Manchester United team – 'The Busby Babes' – decimated by the Munich Air Disaster. It was the year when the EU was formed although back then it was called the European Economic Community. The Leith community travelled to Hampden in large numbers to see if Lawrie Leslie, John Grant, Joe McLelland, Eddie Turnbull, John Paterson, John Baxter, John Fraser, Andy Aitken, Joe Baker, Tommy Preston and Willie Ormond could at long last procure the 'Scottish'. Hibs had beaten Hearts 4–3 at Tynecastle, with all four goals coming from teenage sensation Joe Baker, and they had taken care of Rangers in the semi-final. The feeling among the Hibs support was that the team's name was on the cup. It was not to be. Clyde were a good team then and John Baxter deflected a Johnny Coyle shot past Leslie for the only goal of the game. Baker did get the ball in the net in the second half but the goal was chalked off because he had handled the ball and the hoodoo rolled on.

In 1972, the year in which the British Government imposed direct rule on Northern Ireland, Hibs managed to do a bit of ruling of their own at Hampden. They played six matches there, lost only one of them and lifted the Drybrough Cup and League Cup. Unfortunately, the game that Hibs lost was the Scottish Cup Final against Celtic in May. Hibs' team of Jim Herriot, John Brownlie, Jim Black, John Blackley, Erich Schaedler, Alex Edwards, Pat Stanton, John Hazel, Jimmy O'Rourke, Alan Gordon and Arthur Duncan was, with the exception of Alex Cropley, the combination that became known as Turnbull's Tornadoes. There was genuine optimism that this talented group of players could lift the cup but they lost heavily by six goals to one. In truth, in a very open match, Hibs probably created as many chances as Celtic but, inspired by hat-trick hero Dixie Deans, Jock Stein's men took their opportunities while Eddie Turnbull's side didn't accept theirs. Hibs Hampden heartache had now extended to seventy years.

Hibs had three attempts at beating Rangers in the twice-replayed 1979 Scottish Cup Final. It was the United Nations Year of the Child but yet again it wasn't to be the Year of the Hibernians. An Arthur Duncan headed own goal in the extra time period of the third match was enough to give Rangers the trophy and Jim McArthur, Ally Brazil, George Stewart, Jackie McNamara, Arthur Duncan, Des Bremner, Gordon Rae, Ralph Callachan, Tony Higgins, Ally McLeod and Colin Campbell had proved no more successful than their predecessors of the previous seventy-seven years.

It was a new century and indeed a new millennium when Hibs next rolled up to Hampden on Scottish Cup final day.

The year 2001 will, of course, always be remembered for the terrorist attacks of 11 September, which caused so much suffering in the United States and so much grief throughout the world.

Earlier that year, Hibs, led by the inspirational Frenchman Franck Sauzée, had done their best to stop their Scottish Cup drought stretching to a full hundred years. Once again, Celtic proved too strong at the final stage and there was only disappointment for Nick Colgan, Ian Murray, Paul Fenwick, Gary Smith, Franck Sauzée, Ulrik Laursen, John O'Neill, Grant Brebner, Mathias Jack, Marc Libbra and Mixu Paatelainen and the Hibs support.

In 2012, having only avoided relegation in the last game of the league season, Hibs, under the command of Pat Fenlon, faced Hearts at Hampden in the Scottish Cup final a full 110 years since they had last won it. This was to prove the most depressing final of all as Hearts, with some help from referee Craig Thomson and little resistance from a Hibs team, which included several loan players, inflicted what was for Hibs an unforgettably embarrassing 5–1 defeat. It was a year that Hibs fans and the team – Mark Brown, Mark Docherty, James McPake, Paul Hanlon, Pa Kujabi, Tom Soares, Jorge Claros,

Lewis Stevenson, Isaiah Osbourne, Garry O'Connor and Leigh Griffiths – will want to forget forever.

Fenlon took Hibs back to Hampden twelve months later but it wasn't to prove tenth time lucky as the cup final losing streak reached double figures with Celtic again proving Hibs' nemesis as they won 3–0. Pope Francis had been elected earlier in the year but even the prayers of the Pontiff wouldn't have been enough to save Hibs from defeat so superior was Neil Lennon's team. Ben Williams, Alan Maybury, Jordon Forster, Paul Hanlon, Ryan McGivern, Jorge Claros, Tom Taiwo, Kevin Thomson, Alex Harris, Eoin Doyle and Leigh Griffiths did their best but their best wasn't good enough and Hibs had now gone 111 years without Scottish Cup glory.

So even if the Hibernian team in Alan Stubbs' first season had failed to win promotion and had come up short in its quest to break the club's never-ending Scottish Cup jinx, it wasn't all doom and gloom around Easter Road as season 2014–15 had definitely ended on a much more positive note that it had started.

Hibs had an ambitious and impressive new Chief Executive, a talented young manager presiding over a decent squad of players and backed by a wide-ranging and capable backroom team, and the rift between supporters and the club was in the process of healing.

The forthcoming campaign held out the possibility of promotion if the challenge of Rangers and others could be seen off and the prospect of another tilt at Hibs' personal Holy Grail – the Scottish Cup. Season 2015–16 was to prove an almighty roller coaster ride which ended on the ultimate high. I invite you to join me on my month-by-month journey through a tumultuous period in Hibs' history.

JOURNAL
June 2015 to May 2016

The Ecstasy: Redemption

June 2015

Comings and Goings at Easter Road

Liam Craig moves on – Sheffield United eye Stubbs – Old Firm show interest in Scott Allan – Fyvie, Keatings and Carmichael sign up – Brack family invest in shares

Speaking after Hibs' agonising play-off defeat against Rangers, Alan Stubbs had said that he didn't want to go through the same process at the end of season 2015–16. He made it clear that the club would move quickly in the close season to move players on and bring in new blood. He was as good as his word.

Liam Craig was the first departure and he left Hibs with the utmost dignity. His contract had expired and would not be renewed. Craig said, 'Hibs are a special club with great supporters.' Alan Stubbs responded with, 'Liam is a model professional and has been a great ambassador for Hibs.' That was perfectly true. He had never really replicated his St Johnstone form at Hibs, but he had always given his absolute all. He deserves to have success at his next club. Except when he plays against Hibs, of course!

In another development, David Gray extended his contract by one year and was appointed as club captain for the new season. Interviewed resplendent in Hibs new home kit, he stated, 'It's good to get the white sleeves back.' I am sure that most supporters would agree with that. David displayed tremendous potential in his first few months at Easter Road before he suffered a run of injuries. I hope he will stay fit next season and recapture his previous form.

Sheffield United have sacked their manager Nigel Clough and Alan Stubbs is in the frame to replace him. Stubbs response was, 'I had a big job to do when I took over and it's still a big job. Nothing has changed.'

Rangers are apparently lining up a bid for Scott Allan. It's not hard to know why because Allan is an outstanding game changer of a player. Apparently Burnley too, just relegated from the English Premiership, have been watching Jason Cummings and Dominique Malonga.

Celtic have joined Rangers in trying to sign Scott Allan. They had planned to sign him on a pre-contract in January 2016 and save themselves some money. They are now considering making an earlier move in case Rangers beat them to the punch. This is typical Old Firm arrogance. Not only do they want to cherry-pick other clubs' best players but they also want to do it on the cheap. It really is pathetic.

Andy Murray has strongly refuted allegations that Hibs are mentally weak. Andy has, of course, been accused of mental fragility himself in the past. It hasn't stopped him winning two tennis grand slams and an Olympic gold medal though. Hopefully Hibs can follow the example of their famous supporter and make all their doubters eat their words during season 2015–16.

Next season, Hibs will compete against Rangers again in the Championship. Rangers' new chairman Dave King has promised to invest £20 million in strengthening the Ibrox club. Clearly that makes outright promotion a very hard ask for Hibs.

Alan Stubbs has continued to act swiftly to strengthen Hibs for the promotion challenge ahead. Fraser Fyvie has signed a two-year contract with Hibs. Fyvie combines experience with promise and it is great that he has opted to stay with Hibs rather than go elsewhere. Hibs have also signed James Keatings on a two-year deal. Keatings scored eleven goals for Hearts last season even though he wasn't a regular starter. He scored fifteen goals for Hamilton the season before. He has won promotion from the Championship two years in a row. Now he intends to make it three seasons in succession with Hibs. He also rejected the chance to move to the SPFL Premiership to come to Easter Road.

Both Fyvie and Keatings cited Alan Stubbs as one of the main reasons why they wanted to sign for Hibs. This makes it all the more essential that Hibs move heaven and earth to retain the manager's services.

My daughter Lisa and I have been to Easter Road to hand over our cheques for shares in Hibs. Our commitment to our club continues to grow. Lisa also bought her older son John his first season ticket. He is only three but has already been to three matches and next season he will be at every game with his cousin

Daniel, his mum, his Uncle Pat and myself. That makes me very proud indeed.

Hibs have made another signing. Queen of the South's skilful winger Danny Carmichael has signed a two-year contract, simultaneously weakening Queens and strengthening Hibs. Stubbs has described his early signing swoops as 'a statement of intent'. It certainly is and a very welcome one at that. Even more welcome is the news that Sheffield United have appointed Nigel Adkins as their new manager so they will not be taking Alan Stubbs from Hibs.

July 2015

The Scott Allan Saga Begins

Scott Robertson goes – new contracts for Stevenson, Fontaine, Boyle and Oxley – trip to La Manga – injury for Handling – Rangers appoint Warburton and bid for Allan – Petrofac problems – new deals for management team – marquee signing of McGinn

Scott Robertson has left Hibs. Several players, who were out of contract, have committed to new deals. And there have been further signings. I was sorry to see Robertson go. He was a wholehearted player who worked really hard and was good at doing the unspectacular work on the pitch – the kind that allows the more skilful players to flourish. He even contributed a few goals last season. Hibs did make 'Robbo' an offer to stay but he claimed that it was on significantly reduced terms and turned it down. He stated that he was very sad to be leaving Easter Road. A lot of fans will miss his commitment to the cause. Robertson has signed for a team in Romania and will live there on his own while his family remain in Dundee. It seems a strange career move and it wouldn't be a surprise if he was back in Scottish football sooner rather than later.

Lewis Stevenson, Liam Fontaine, Martin Boyle and Mark Oxley have all committed their futures to Hibs. It's very good news that Stevenson and Fontaine will continue their involvement with the club. They are both excellent players. Boyle has pace, is versatile and is a valuable squad member. The case for signing Oxley is less clear-cut. Big Mark was pretty unconvincing for much of last season and he has a lot to prove.

Alan Stubbs' busy summer continues and he has made two more signings. He has brought in a defensive midfielder in Marvin Bartley. Marvin is twenty-nine and six foot three. He has played for Bournemouth, Burnley and Leyton Orient and has been described by Alan Stubbs as a 'ball winner'. A back-up goalkeeper in thirty-three-year-old Spaniard Antonio Reguero has also arrived at Easter Road. Reguero failed to hold down a first team starting place at his previous Scottish clubs – Inverness, Kilmarnock and Ross County – so the jury is very much still out on what he will bring to the party.

Hibs have been in La Manga for a week's hot-weather training. Given that the club has a state-of-the-art training centre and we are at the height of summer at home, was this a necessary use of club funds, which are at a premium? Alan Stubbs insists that it was. The players trained three times daily in temperatures which were at times around 100°F and the manager is adamant that they will be super-fit when the new season gets underway. Unfortunately, James Keating picked up a hamstring strain in Spain and has been sidelined ever since. Farid El Alagui, Martin Boyle and Danny Carmichael didn't travel to the training camp at all as they are recovering from previous injuries.

Hibs have played three pre-season friendly matches to date. They lost 2–1 to Wigan in La Manga and since returning have beaten Berwick Rangers 3–0 at Shielfield Park and Dunfermline 2–1 at East End Park. Scott Allan was outstanding in both matches. There are several clubs who are keen to sign him but Allan has so far insisted that he is committed to seeing out the final year of his contract with Hibs. Let's hope he does as he is the best player in the Championship by a long way and could be the difference between Hibs being promoted or spending another year in the second tier of Scottish football.

Danny Handling has sadly picked up a serious knee injury in the pre-season friendly match at Berwick which will sideline him for most of the coming season which is a blow to both the club and the player.

Rangers have appointed a new manager, Mark Warburton, who has joined them from Brentford along with his assistant Davie Weir. Rangers will start their season by travelling to Easter Road to play Hibs in the Petrofac Training Cup. Warburton has stated that the match against Hibs is not a source of concern to him on the basis that 'It's not Real Madrid we're playing after all.'

My daughter Lisa and I received our share certificates at the weekend. We are absolutely delighted to have them and to be in the position of owning even an infinitesimal part of the club we love. I took mine to an art workshop to be framed today and will hang it in my study with my other Hibs artwork when I collect it at the end of the week.

Rangers have made two bids for Scott Allan. They initially offered the derisory amount of £175,000, which was no more than a calculated insult, and then upped their figure to £250,000. Leeann Dempster described the bids as 'unwelcome' and Alan Stubbs has advised Allan to see his contract out and take his pick of any interested clubs, including those from the English Premiership, at the end of the season. Stubbs quite rightly pointed out that the timing of Rangers' offers, coming as they did, two days before the clubs meet on Saturday, is no coincidence.

There has been a further development on the Scott Allan front with STV reporting that he has informed Hibs that he wants to leave to join Rangers.

I collected my framed Hibs shares certificate today. It is now on my study wall below a photograph of Keith Wright, Chris Reid and myself holding the Skol Cup. The photograph was taken in early 1992 when then director Tom O'Malley brought Keith and Chris to the school where I was the headteacher.

Also on my study walls are photographs of Joe Baker and Gordon Smith scoring for Hibs. Gordon's goal was against Hearts on 2 January 1950. The crowd that day, over 60,000, was Hibs' record attendance.

Rangers have beaten Hibs 6–2 in the Petrofac Training Cup which hardly represents an ideal start to the season. It was a strange game. Hibs played a very young team, which included teenagers Jason Cummings, Scott Martin and Lewis Allan as well as Jordon Forster, Sam Stanton and Fraser Fyvie who are in their early twenties.

Rangers looked really fit, pressed Hibs incessantly when they were in possession and passed the ball crisply. They were helped by some inept defending from Hibs. Two of their new signings right-back James Tavernier and striker Martyn Waghorn scored and looked impressive.

Alan Stubbs decided to leave Scott Allan on the bench but said after the match that Allan is going nowhere. Allan was outstanding when he came on and is an absolutely vital player for Hibs. After the match Stubbs described the result as a 'kick up the backside'.

Farid El Alagui and Martin Boyle are still recuperating from surgery and Danny Carmichael and James Keating have picked up injuries in pre-season training. Marvin Bartley is not match-fit yet and both Dominique Malonga and Jordan Forster went off injured today. When everyone is fit, Hibs will be able to field a much stronger and more experienced team than that which ended the game today.

There have been more developments in the Scott Allan transfer saga. Allan has now submitted a written transfer request. Hibs have responded by issuing a statement reiterating that Allan will not be sold to Rangers. That is positive. Less encouraging is the implication that he might be sold to someone else.

Allan should take a good look at himself. He is under contract to Hibs, has previously expressed how happy he is at Easter Road and now he is doing everything he can to secure a move. He is behaving very poorly indeed. He is on record in a number of television and newspaper interviews declaring how much he owes Hibs and Alan Stubbs for getting his career back on track and stating that he wants to stay and help Hibs win promotion. Now without batting an eyelid, he is going back on all of that. Where is your integrity, Scott?

Bookmakers had made Alan Stubbs favourite to be the first Scottish Championship manager to leave his job during season

2015–16. They had cut the odds on this happening to 3–1 based on a belief that if the Hibs board, despite all their protestations to the contrary, transferred Scott Allan to Rangers, Stubbs would walk away from Easter Road. Well, that is one bet which must now be off as Stubbs and his coaches, John Doolan and Andy Holden, have extended their contracts with Hibs to the end of season 2016–17 which is very good news for the club and its supporters.

Alan Stubbs is not yet the finished article as a manager but he has done an excellent job so far and has the potential to do even better in future. Hibs need continuity and stability, and these contract extensions give them both these things.

Hibs have confirmed that they have signed John McGinn from St Mirren on a four-year contract. Alan Stubbs has made it clear that the club paid a 'significant' compensation fee for the player and described the signing as a 'statement of intent'. McGinn is a player who has already made a century of first-team appearances by the age of twenty and Hibs should be applauded for investing in his promise. This is a major piece of business.

The Glasgow press have, in my opinion, favoured Rangers and the player in the whole Scott Allan saga. They clearly expected Hibs to cave in and sell Allan to Rangers quite quickly. Now that that hasn't happened, they are pursuing other lines.

At his press conference on Thursday, they reminded Alan Stubbs that he had asked for a transfer while a player at Bolton. Their implication being that Stubbs' stance on holding on to Allan was therefore hypocritical. Our manager soon put them in their place. He reminded them that when Bolton refused his request to move, he knuckled down and played another full season. He added that when he did move, the club received £4 million from Celtic for his services so the two situations are hardly comparable.

August 2015

The Scott Allan Saga Ends

League Cup progress – defeat at Dumbarton – Allan signs for Celtic – Henderson and McGeouch arrive – setback at Ibrox – Darren McGregor joins up

Hibs have comfortably taken care of Paul Hegarty's Montrose to progress to the next round of the League Cup. Montrose were ultra-defensive. It is not uncommon for teams to deploy ten men behind the ball but on a regular basis today, all eleven Montrose players were between the ball and their own goal.

Hibs' goals came from the very promising teenager Scott Martin, Scott Allan and Jason Cummings, who was celebrating his 20th birthday. Scott Allan again started the match on the bench and when he came on, he was head and shoulders above anyone else on the pitch.

It was a very young Hibs team as Martin and Cummings were joined by Sam Stanton – who played very well – and Alex

Harris. Teenage substitutes Oli Shaw and Jordan Sinclair also came on to play their part.

Marvin Bartley made his debut and was very effective at winning the ball and then making a simple and effective pass. When Allan came on his reception was predominantly positive although there was the occasional boo from those who take exception to his transfer request. He opened the Montrose defence at will though and made it clear why Hibs badly need to keep him this season.

The West of Scotland media has kept up its relentless pressure on Hibs and Alan Stubbs over the Scott Allan affair. The *Sunday Mail* has made contact with a senior figure in the Bolton Wanderers Supporters' Association who, according to the newspaper, has branded Alan Stubbs a 'hypocrite'. He says that when Stubbs wanted to leave Bolton, he went out of his way to disconnect from what was going on at the club and alienated the fans. Stubbs tells a rather different story.

Former Rangers player, Alex Rae, has claimed that £225,000 is a fair price for Allan and says that he fears for the player's state of mind. What parallel universe is he living in?

Rangers have made a third bid of £280,000 for Scott Allan and Rotherham United are reported to have offered £375,000 for the playmaker. Hibs have rejected both bids. It is reported that Rangers plan to return with a fourth bid for Allan.

This is all very unsettling for Hibs but they must stick to their guns and not let Allan go to Ibrox under any circumstances. He should also start the match against Dumbarton on Saturday, irrespective of his state of mind.

Hibs are considering signing non-league striker Jamie Insall from Stourbridge. He is twenty-three and a proverbial goal machine – he scored sixty-seven goals in one season – at non-league level. He also has a conviction for breaking an opponent's jaw on his record. He received a suspended jail sentence for this offence in 2011. Alan Stubbs sees him as a rough diamond with development potential. It's certainly an interesting signing.

Hibernian Football Club turned 140 years old on 6 August 2015. A very happy birthday to the team formed by Irish immigrants in the parish of St Patrick's in Edinburgh's Cowgate. The team which was recognised as unofficial champion of the world in the nineteenth century, which had won two Scottish Cups by 1902 (although sadly none since), which was the first British team to compete in the European Cup and the first Scottish team to install floodlights, which was represented by great teams like the Famous Five and Turnbull's Tornadoes which may now reside in Scottish football's second tier but can be proud of its history and positive about its future. Let's hope that that future commences with a victory in the first league game of the season at Dumbarton and ends with a Scottish Cup win in May.

Hibs' promotion campaign has got off to a disastrous start with a 2–1 defeat at Dumbarton. There was a huge element of déjà vu from last season about this defeat. Hibs dominated the game and missed chances while Dumbarton – with much less of the ball and significantly fewer opportunities – managed to score two goals.

Both the Sons' goals came from carelessly conceded free kicks and the best Hibs could do in reply was a goal from Dominique Malonga. All in all, it was a desperately disappointing result.

There was more disappointment for Hibs with the news that Celtic have entered the race to sign Scott Allan. They are reported to have offered £500,000 and two players – Dylan

McGeouch and Liam Henderson – both of whom are young and talented.

If Hibs keep Allan until the end of the current transfer window, the speculation on his future will die down until December and then start up all over again. He will then sign a pre-contract agreement with Rangers on 1 January and be a dead man walking with the Hibs support for the rest of the season. When he subsequently leaves Easter Road next summer, Hibs will get nothing in return. Although my original instinct was for Hibs not to sell Allan, given the way things have developed, it makes far more sense to rid the club of the ongoing disruption and speculation around his presence.

If Allan manages to overcome his devotion to all things Ibrox and sign on for Celtic, what will the Rangers fans who sang 'Scott Allan, he's one of our own' during the recent Petrofac Training Cup tie at Easter Road make of it I wonder?

Scott Allan has now signed a four-year contract with Celtic and brought to an end several weeks of upheaval around Easter Road. Disappointingly, the actual fee paid to Hibs was much less than the figure speculated previously. Hibs have apparently received only £275,000 plus Liam Henderson and possibly Dylan McGeouch. The highly promising Henderson has joined on a one-year loan deal. It is believed that Hibs and McGeouch are still negotiating. The conjecture is that Hibs want McGeouch on a four-year contract and, apparently, he is only prepared to agree to a two-year deal. If McGeouch doesn't sign, you have to assume that Hibs will receive additional cash.

Hibs are off the mark in the league after beating Morton 1–0 at Easter Road. It was a victory but a far from convincing one. Jason Cummings who, surprisingly, was left on the bench, came on after fifty-eight minutes to score the winning goal with his first touch. Liam Henderson came on as a substitute too and made a good impression. John McGinn and Danny Carmichael also made their home debuts. McGinn was far and away the more impressive of the two. Hibs' least effective player by a long way was Dominique Malonga, who looked uninterested and missed two gilt-edged chances.

Earlier in the day, I had attended an Edinburgh Festival speaking event with the great journalist and broadcaster Hugh McIlvanney. I had got to know Hugh when he wrote a superb introduction to Lawrie Reilly's autobiography, which I co-authored. Hugh was kind enough to invite me to join him and his family for lunch afterwards but, being the football man he is, when I explained that I had to get Easter Road, he fully understood and wished both me and Hibs well.

Hibs travel to Ibrox for their next league fixture to face a Rangers team that has made a highly impressive start to the season under their new manager Mark Warburton. Alan Stubbs acknowledged this week that Warburton was doing well, then stated that it wasn't difficult to do well when you had lots of money to spend. This will no doubt fire up Warburton even more before they clash at the weekend.

Mark Warburton has reacted to Alan Stubbs' remarks about his 'easy job' by telling the Hibs boss to 'keep his mouth shut'. Riling the Rangers manager before Sunday's Hibs vs. Rangers match may not prove to have been the wisest of moves on Stubbs' part. He may have been angry with Rangers because they have followed their orchestrated campaign to unsettle Scott Allan by poaching Hibs' Head of Fitness and Sports Science, Craig Flannigan. Clearly they must be offering Flannigan more money than Hibs are currently paying him, which explains why Alan

Stubbs made the point about Mark Warburton having money to spend.

Dylan McGeouch has finally signed for Hibs. He has put pen to paper on a three-year contract. He didn't seem exactly euphoric when he was interviewed on Hibs TV but I don't think he is a naturally effusive person. I am sure too that he is a dyed-in-the-wool Celtic man and would have preferred to stay at Parkhead. However, Celtic clearly don't want him and Hibs do so he is a Hibee now. I am pleased that this is the case as he is a very good player and once he gets used to the idea that his time at Parkhead is up, he should be an excellent addition to the Hibs squad.

Alex Harris has been sent out on loan to Queen of the South. When Harris first broke into the Hibs team under Pat Fenlon, he looked an outstanding prospect. Sadly since breaking his ankle two years ago, he has avoided physical contact, been reluctant to take defenders on and seemed a shadow of his former self.

Hibs have lost 1–0 to Rangers at Ibrox. They didn't deserve to. Alan Stubbs set Hibs up to be hard to break down and to play on the counter attack. They did this very effectively and created four clear-cut chances. Two fell to Jason Cummings and the other two went to Liam Henderson. None were converted.

Rangers scored direct from a free kick in the second half. James Tavernier, who curled a superb dead ball finish past Mark Oxley in the recent Petrofac Training Cup match, repeated the dose here. It was a beautifully flighted shot but the award should never have been given. Kenny Miller drove the ball against Dylan McGeouch from point blank range. The ball struck McGeouch's leg and went from there on to his hand. The contact between ball and hand was clearly unintentional yet referee

Steven McLean, who was otherwise excellent, gave Rangers a direct free kick, which resulted in the match-winning goal.

After the game, Rangers captain Lee Wallace was interviewed on Sky Sports. He launched into an astonishingly arrogant rant about how good Rangers were and didn't draw breath for at least three minutes. During his impassioned monologue he said that Rangers had been 'brought down to Hibs' level' on a couple of occasions during the match. How dare he? Rangers were fortunate to win and Hibs certainly don't need someone like Wallace patronising them. If I was Alan Stubbs, I would play the tape of motor-mouth Wallace's interview to the Hibs squad at the earliest opportunity. It would be sure to serve as a real motivation for the rest of the season.

Hibs had some first-class performances. John McGinn was outstanding in midfield and Jason Cummings was razor sharp up front. Unfortunately, the team yet again failed to convert a number of excellent chances.

There has been some interesting news from Ibrox. Darren McGregor has left Rangers by mutual consent. McGregor was Rangers' Player of the Year last year, he is only thirty, an excellent centre half and a Hibs supporter. He has had serious injuries in the past but has stayed fit in recent seasons. Alan Stubbs should think seriously about signing him.

Hibs have indeed moved quickly to sign Darren McGregor on a two-year deal. His delight at joining the team he has followed since boyhood was transparently obvious and totally genuine. If Darren kisses his Hibs badge on scoring, he will most definitely mean it. I just hope that he can stay fit.

Hibs have beaten Stranraer 1–0 to progress to the next round of the League Cup. It was a mightily unimpressive performance with the only goal coming when a Stranraer player diverted the ball into his own net in the second half. Hibs were even more toothless than usual and are still having severe difficulty in breaking down inferior teams which are well organised, disciplined and set up in an ultra-defensive formation.

Dylan McGeouch was outstanding, John McGinn wasn't far behind and Darren McGregor was impressively combative but no one else made a great contribution. Liam Henderson and Jason Cummings again missed chances, and Henderson is clearly still finding his feet.

At the moment, Hibs are guilty of making far too many square passes and putting careless final balls into the box. Last night helped explain why Hibs lost to Dumbarton in their opening fixture. If teams are massed in defence, maintain their concentration and hold their shape, then Hibs just don't score enough goals against them which inevitably leads to draws and defeats.

Hibs have beaten Raith Rovers 2–0 at Easter Road to end the month on a winning note. James Keatings – on debut – and Jason Cummings scored the goals and the victory was relatively comfortable. Raith are a strong, physical team with a threat up front in Jon Daly but Hibs handled them well. The only disappointing feature was that after scoring their second goal, Hibs played cautiously holding on to what they had rather than looking to extend their lead.

Dylan McGeouch and John McGinn were again outstanding in midfield and Keatings and Cummings gelled well up front. Mark Oxley also made a couple of decent saves.

At full time, Alan Stubbs gave Jason Cummings a ticking off as he came off the pitch. I can only presume this was because

Cummings tried to score from a tight angle late in the game when he could have rolled the ball across goal to provide an easy finish for Dominique Malonga, who was on as a substitute. After the game, Stubbs spoke about Cummings needing to judge how he played on his overall performance rather than just being concerned with how many goals he scored. He did add that Cummings' attitude was typical of good strikers.

Hibs organised a 'Hibs Kids Parade' for their youngest supporters before the Raith game. It was a real pleasure to join my daughter Lisa and her three-year-old season ticket holder son John on a walk round the track as the players warmed up prior to kick off. As if that wasn't an exciting enough experience, we got to meet Sunshine the Leith Lynx as well!

Rangers have made a relentless start to the season. They beat previously undefeated Queen of the South 5–1 at Palmerston Park on Sunday to maintain their 100% record. Queens played most of the second half with ten men after a controversial sending off and two of Rangers' goals came from penalties.

With six points out of twelve, Hibs are three points better off than they were this time last season. They will have to wait for their next match due to the forthcoming international break which features Jason Cummings and John McGinn playing for Scotland's Under 21s.

September 2015

League Cup Heroics

Loan signings – gathering momentum in the league – League Cup victory over Aberdeen – slip up against Saints

The summer transfer window has now closed and Hibs have done two pieces of late business.

Striker Henri Anier has come in on loan from Dundee United. Anier is an Estonian international and, as a big, powerful front man, is a contrast to the type of strikers Hibs have at present. Anier, who has also played in Germany and for Motherwell, has failed to set the heather on fire during his time at Tannadice. Alan Stubbs clearly sees something in him that is not apparent to his current manager Jackie McNamara.

More excitingly, Hibs have also signed Islam Feruz on loan from Chelsea. Feruz is a naturalised Scot who came to this country from Somalia. Originally on Celtic's books, he was a prodigy who played in age groups above his chronological age and performed impressively. When he was sixteen, he turned his back on Celtic and signed for Chelsea who had to pay a £300,000 development fee.

He hasn't broken through at Stamford Bridge and has had two unsuccessful loan spells in Greece and at Blackpool. His record at various age group levels up to Under 21s for Scotland is good.

Feruz, who is only five foot four, clearly has talent but seems to be hard to handle. Alan Stubbs has demonstrated his man-management skills before so let's hope he can keep Feruz on board at Easter Road and get the best out of an undoubtedly talented striker who is still not quite twenty years old.

Hibs have had a busy summer window. Tomas Cerny, Liam Craig, Scott Robertson, Scott Allan, Lewis Allan (loan) and Alex Harris (loan) have all left Easter Road while Mark Oxley, Fraser Fyvie, Lewis Stevenson and Liam Fontaine have signed new deals after their original contracts expired. Antonio Reguero, Darren McGregor, Marvin Bartley, Danny Carmichael, John McGinn, Dylan McGeouch and James Keatings are new signings while Liam Henderson, Henri Anier and Islam Feruz have joined on loan. It remains to be seen whether the revamped Hibs squad can get the club back to the Premier League where it belongs and, even better, attain the long awaited dream of capturing the Holy Grail which is the Scottish Cup. What a magical achievement that would be.

Hibs have signed their third striker in twenty-four hours. Jamie Insall has been handed a three-year contract. Twenty-three-year-old Midlander Insall has been on trial at Easter Road for a month. Although he has only ever played non-league football, he has a phenomenal goal scoring record. Can he make the step up to the senior game? Alan Stubbs obviously thinks that he can.

Rangers have taken advantage of Hibs' inactivity, due to international commitments, to beat Raith Rovers 5–0. James Tavernier unbelievably scored again – he must be the most prolific right back in the history of football. Rangers also converted two penalties for the second week in a row. With fifteen points from five games they are in danger of replicating Hearts' performance last season and running away with the league.

While that action was taking place, my daughter Lisa, my youngest son Kevin and my grandson John and I were at the Hibernian Clubstore at Easter Road. Lisa had ordered a new home strip for John as soon as the new kit was unveiled. However, it has taken until now for the home shirt in John's size to become available. Neil, the manager in the club store who is a very nice man, phoned Lisa to say that John's strip was in.

We headed straight down to the ground and collected John's shirt and shorts (the socks still weren't available) and headed home. When we came into Lisa's back garden through her rear gate, all the family, who were sitting in the sunshine after lunch, gave John a big clap as he ran onto the grass, resplendent in his new strip. There was a major lump in my throat.

Alan Stubbs has agreed to Derek Riordan training with Hibs. He has stated that the purpose is to allow Riordan to regain his fitness but he hasn't entirely ruled out the possibility of a deal at a later date. I, for one, would be delighted to see Deek back at Easter Road for a third spell with the club. He is only thirty-two and won't have lost his ability. It is just a matter of whether he is prepared to make the commitment to get himself fully fit. He certainly deserves a better stage for his talents than the succession of lower-league clubs he has played with in recent years.

Islam Feruz told the media at the start of the week that he intended to turn over a new leaf and learn from his previous mistakes. In the early hours of Wednesday morning he was arrested for allegedly driving his £80,000 Porsche without a licence or insurance and will appear in court in February of next year. It was also reported that he gave the police a false name when they stopped him. Not the most encouraging of starts to his Hibs career for an undoubtedly talented footballer, who was described in one of the newspapers as 'Bad Boy Feruz'.

Another player to whom the 'bad boy' tag has been applied in the past is Leigh Griffiths. Leigh has been in court as a consequence of his standing on a chair in a pub after a Hibs vs. Hearts match last season and singing a less than politically correct song about Rudi Skácel (a ditty that the aforementioned Mr Riordan has also vocalised in the past). Due to his apology and recent excellent behaviour, Leigh was merely admonished. He has played brilliantly for Celtic this season but it would be fantastic to see him back in the green and white of Hibs some time soon.

Rangers chairman Dave King, who has shown no sign to date of splashing out the £20 million that he had talked about spending earlier, claimed this week that Hibs had initially approached the Ibrox club about selling Scott Allan to them. Leeann Dempster immediately refuted his claim. I know whose version of events I believe.

Scott Robertson's time in Romania has come to an abrupt end. Three months after agreeing his deal there, he has ripped up his contract by mutual consent and returned home. It was a transfer that was never likely to go well and I feel sorry for 'Robbo' who was such a wholehearted player for Hibs. I am sure that he will get a new club in Scotland soon.

Somebody who has already been fixed up with a new team to play for is former Hearts left-back Adam Eckersley who has signed on at Easter Road until January 2016. I liked Eckersley as a player when he was at Tynecastle. He was fast and aggressive and he will provide cover and competition for Lewis Stevenson who has made a slow start to the season.

With the international break over, it is time to return to league action. Hibs are at home to Alloa in a game that they simply have to win. In fact, it would be nice if Hibs didn't just win but for once scored a few goals, notched up a convincing victory and saved their long-suffering supporters from spending the last fifteen minutes biting their nails after a plethora of missed opportunities earlier in the game.

Hibs beat Alloa convincingly and comfortably by three goals to nil. In truth, Hibs could easily have notched double figures. The game followed a familiar pattern for Championship games at Easter Road. Alloa placed ten men behind the ball, worked extremely hard and defended as if their lives depended on it. Hibs passed the ball well and contrived to miss lots of chances. Thankfully Liam Henderson, Jason Cummings and John McGinn all eventually managed to get on the score sheet. Henderson and McGinn's goals were their first for the club.

McGinn, Marvin Bartley and Dylan McGeouch were all excellent in midfield. McGinn looks like an excellent player. Islam Feruz and Dominique Malonga came on as second-half substitutes. Neither was particularly impressive. The one negative note was a recurrence of James Keatings' hamstring injury.

Keatings had again looked sharp and will be missed during his latest absence.

Elsewhere, Rangers won again beating Livingston 3–0 at Ibrox. They have a 100% win record under Mark Warburton and are threatening to run away with the title. Hibs have the squad to win every week as well and must continue to do so. Falkirk have made a great start to the season winning four and drawing one of their first five games. Their latest win was away to Ian Murray's St Mirren. The Bairns were 2–0 down at half time but came back to win 3–2 and claim second spot in the league, four points ahead of Hibs in third place. Peter Houston certainly knows how to get the best out of his players. Queen of the South, having won their first three matches, have now lost two in a row.

Hibs kept their momentum going by beating Livingston 1–0, but they made hard work of it. Still the victory at what is no longer known as Almondvale but is now called the Tony Macaroni Arena (the grounds in the Championship certainly have some distinctive names) was Hibs' first away win of the season. Liam Henderson scored a lovely goal direct from a free kick and Hibs should have been out of sight by half time. Livingston came more into the game in the second half and Hibs were happy in the end to leave with the points. Alan Stubbs said after the game that sometimes you have to just grind out a result. He was right and it's a pity that the team didn't do exactly that in the first game of the season at Dumbarton.

Hibs are about to switch their attention to the League Cup where they will meet Aberdeen at Easter Road. The Dons have a 100% domestic record this season and sit at the top of the Scottish Premiership, a clear five points in front of Celtic whom they recently defeated.

Last night Rangers lost for the first time this season when St Johnstone ran out 3–1 winners in a League Cup tie at Ibrox.

Saints defended resolutely and in numbers and were clinical on the counter attack. On another night, Rangers might have won the game, which suggests that the gap between the Premiership and the Championship is not that big, as does the fact that Morton knocked out Motherwell. On the other hand, Ross County, who have become a formidable team, demolished Falkirk by a humiliating 7–0 score line. That is an astounding score line, given Falkirk's normal level of resolution and resilience.

Hibs fans were treated to what was by far their team's best match of the season, as a disciplined and focused performance inflicted on Aberdeen their first defeat in Scottish football since the current campaign got underway in early August and, in the process, secured qualification for the League Cup quarter-final.

Alan Stubbs went with three central defenders, and Darren McGregor, Paul Hanlon and Liam Fontaine were all outstanding. Wing-backs David Gray and Lewis Stevenson bombed forward on a regular basis but defended well too. The consequence was that Mark Oxley was rarely tested.

In midfield, Dylan McGeouch and John McGinn were their usual industrious, excellent selves and were well backed up by Liam Henderson and then Danny Carmichael when he came on for Henderson in the second half. Up front, Martin Boyle put in a committed shift while Jason Cummings also worked tirelessly.

Cummings gave Hibs the lead in the eighty-second minute with a brilliant, curling left-foot shot. Not everyone was delighted when Alan Stubbs then took Jason off and replaced him with Dominique Malonga. The manager had noticed that Cummings was suffering from cramp. Malonga then confounded his critics (and those who are critical of him find fault with his effort not his ability) by scoring an amazing solo goal to seal a famous victory. Big Dom slalomed through the middle, wrong footing three Dons defenders as he went, before planting an unstoppable finish into the bottom right-hand corner of the net. It was a goal which Pele or Maradona would have been proud of. The atmosphere at the game was vibrant and noisy, and brought back memories of vintage Easter Road evenings. Hopefully Hibs can carry this form into the next league game against St Mirren.

Unfortunately, Hibs midweek exertions caught up with them when St Mirren came to Easter Road and a leg weary side, lacking any kind of zip or energy, could do no better than draw 1–1. An avoidable goal was conceded and gilt-edged chances were passed up. Nothing new to report there then.

Rangers beat Morton 4–0 at Cappielow (they got yet another penalty and the incredible scoring right-back James Tavernier was on target again) and they are now way ahead of Hibs in the Championship. Already Hibs look to be playing for second place.

We learned today that Henri Anier has joined Islam Feruz, James Keatings and Farid El Alagui on the injury list. Only Hibs could have seven first team strikers and find four of them injured at the same time.

Hibs have drawn Dundee United in the quarter-finals of the Scottish League Cup. It is a home tie and brings back memories of last season's competition when Hibs lost on penalties to United at the same stage of the tournament. In that game, Matt Kennedy had the opportunity to put Hibs into the semi-finals by converting his spot kick. He lost his nerve and hit a soft shot straight to the goalkeeper and Hibs ended up going out.

Dundee United will have a new manager this time around as Jackie McNamara who started so well at Tannadice has been relieved of his duties following his team's recent prolonged slump. McNamara won't be walking away a poor man as he received a cut of the big-money transfer deals that have significantly reduced United debts in recent times. He has also been given a severance payment.

Various names are in the frame to replace McNamara. They include Mixu Paatelainen, Jim McIntyre, who has done a terrific job at Ross County, Tommy Wright, who has won the Scottish Cup with St Johnstone, and Stuart McCall who, of course, left Rangers when Mark Warburton was appointed. Whoever is in the Tangerines' dugout when the match comes around, Hibs have the squad to win the game and progress to the last four.

October 2015

A Winning Month

Dundee United show interest in Stubbs – new look for West Stand – Authors' Night at St Pat's – Championship consistency

The *Daily Mail* has claimed that Dundee United want Alan Stubbs to be their next manager. I can understand United wanting Stubbs but I would be surprised and disappointed if he decided to leave Hibs for Tannadice. Hibs have bigger crowds than United despite playing in a lower league. United also sell all their best players and their chairman Steven Thomson handed a letter to Jackie McNamara telling him he was dismissed from his post after the United vs. St Johnstone match last Saturday, which hardly suggests that he would be the ideal chairman to work for.

Former Hibs boss Terry Butcher has already been sacked by Newport County. He only took up his post in April and he leaves the Welsh side at the bottom of League 2. Butcher did really well at Inverness before coming to Easter Road, but his performances since then have been very poor indeed.

Alan Stubbs has commented on the links in the media between himself and Dundee United. He spoke about having a job to do to at Hibs and the fact that that situation hadn't changed.

In the meantime, Stubbs' focus has to be on Hibs and the need for a win in Dumfries in the upcoming game against Queen of the South. The artificial pitch will be a problem as, no doubt, will Hibs' continuing failure to convert chances into goals. Queens' impressive young manager James Fowler is about to celebrate his first anniversary as team boss. Let's hope he doesn't have a victory to celebrate as well.

Hibs afforded their fans the luxury of a rare comfortable victory by beating Queen of the South 3–0 at Palmerston Park with goals from Jason Cummings (his seventh of the season), Liam Henderson and Martin Boyle. That is the kind of result Hibs should be achieving regularly in the Championship given the disparity in both quantity and quality between our squad and the more limited resources of most other teams in the league. Dominique Malonga and Lewis Stevenson both played particularly well. Alan Stubbs made Malonga his man of the match. Stubbs wasn't entirely pleased with his team's display, though. He considered their second-half performance to be 'complacent'.

After the ridiculous defeat to Dumbarton in the first game of the season and the two points thrown away to St Mirren at home recently, it is hard to believe that Hibs still haven't got rid of the tendency to relax and not be sufficiently ruthless in matches – a habit which cost them so dearly last season and has hurt them again in the early part of the current campaign.

Rangers have won their ninth successive league game beating Falkirk 3–1 at Ibrox. They scored twice in the last eight minutes to seal the points. Their crucial second goal came from a disputed free kick on the edge of the Falkirk penalty box scored by James Tavernier (who else?). The Bairns manager, Peter Houston, was incandescent. He was certain that former Hibee Tom Taiwo had won the ball and hadn't fouled the Rangers player. I am not so sure. I think he got a bit of both ball and man and I could see where the referee, John McKendrick, was coming from. Houston made his feelings clear to the official and has been reported to the SFA.

Hibs now sit in third position in the Championship. They are way behind Rangers and one point behind Raith Rovers who are going really well under Ray McKinnon. St Mirren could only draw at home to Alloa, which puts Hibs' failure to beat them last week firmly into perspective.

Hibs have unveiled a new look to the entrance to the main stand at the West of the stadium. The club crest has been mounted in two places on the exterior of the stand and 'Hibernian Football Club' is now emblazoned along the top of the stand. It looks great and gives the main entrance a classy appearance while creating much more of a Hibernian feel to the centrepiece of our ground. Well done to the board for taking this step. Frank Dougan was the director who was quoted in the media about this move and, if Frank was the man responsible for this happening, he deserves great credit for it.

Dundee United have approached St Johnstone for permission to speak to their manager Tommy Wright. St Johnstone have stated that there is absolutely no chance of Wright leaving Mac-Diarmid Park. It will be interesting to see if they maintain their position. Mixu Paatelainen, Stuart McCall and former West Brom boss Alan Irvine are also being mentioned in dispatches. United's reported interest in Alan Stubbs seems to have cooled for the moment. Long may that continue to be the case.

Dundee United have accepted that St Johnstone do not intend to allow Tommy Wright to leave them and have turned their interest elsewhere. Meanwhile Brentford in the English Championship have parted company with their manager and Alan Stubbs, according to the press, is firmly on their radar. It seems that every time a manager moves on or is sacked, Stubbs is linked with the vacancy. I know he will depart for pastures new at some stage but I really hope that he isn't going anywhere just yet.

Dundee United's search for a new team manager is not proving straightforward. They have now had their advances for John Hughes spurned by Inverness Caledonian Thistle. Hughes has done really well in the Highlands but he was a major disappointment in the final part of his spell as Hibs manager which was a real let down for all Hibees who very much wanted him to succeed. It will be very interesting to see who United approach next.

Jason Cummings and John McGinn have played two games each for Scotland's Under 21 side during the international break, which has just come to an end. John captained the team that lost to France and drew with Iceland. Hopefully both players have come through these matches without injury and will be fit to face Dumbarton at Easter Road when league business resumes.

Mixu Paatelainen has been confirmed as the new manager of Dundee United so it doesn't look as if Alan Stubbs is going anywhere just yet, which is good. Stubbs himself has been in bullish mood telling the media that he still believed that Hibs can win the Scottish Championship. He was backed up by James Keatings, who said that he expects Rangers to falter at some stage of the season. I hope that they are both right. For them to be so, Hibs have to win every game starting with the visit of Dumbarton.

Former Hibee Derek Riordan has been in the news for the wrong reasons. He was fined £400 for headbutting a 'person unknown' in a bar in the Grassmarket just before Christmas last year. Reading the reports of this incident, it sounds like much has been made of little. The police haven't been able to identify the other man involved in the altercation and no complaint was made to them. The 'victim' was apparently taunting Riordan and after a heated exchange, he put his face very close to the man's face. After that CCTV footage showed that Riordan's head made light contact with the other man's face. Riordan's legal representative confirmed in court that he was currently training with a prominent Scottish football club in the hope of winning a contract. I hope that Hibs allow him to continue training at East Mains, that he sticks at it and that he does indeed win a contract for what would be a third spell at Easter Road.

Tonight I took part in a question and answer session at the St Patrick's Branch of the Hibs Supporters' Association at the clubrooms in Sunnyside Lane. It was an 'Authors' Night' and I was joined by Bobby Sinnott and Ian Colquhoun. Bobby is a leading Hibs statistician and wrote *The Hibernian Miscellany*. He and Ian have recently collaborated on a book called *Hibernian on this Day* which recounts notable Hibernian incidents and results throughout their history for every day of the year. It was a really good night with some excellent questions and chat.

As a branch, St Pat's have done some really good things. They have had busts made of Canon Hannan and Michael Whelehan, have had a headstone erected in Easter Road cemetery for former manager Dan McMichael and a commemorative plaque unveiled in St Patrick's church. They have donated Hibs season tickets to children who would otherwise not be able to afford them and were instrumental in the recent celebrations of Hibs' 140th anniversary and the accompanying production of a retro strip bearing the harp badge to mark that special occasion. All credit to them.

Hibs have defeated Dumbarton 4–2. They were great going forward. Dominique Malonga scored a special goal – an exquisite curling shot into the goalkeeper's top left-hand corner – and James Keating, on his return from injury, contributed another excellent finish. Liam Fontaine with a header and Jason Cummings from the penalty spot scored the other two goals.

Defensively, things were a whole lot less impressive. David Gray sliced a clearance straight to a Dumbarton attacker for the first goal and Mark Oxley didn't help matters by attempting to save the ball with his feet and failing dismally to do so. The Sons' second goal came from a header from a free kick and again Oxley was far too easily beaten.

Hibs now face a midweek trip to Falkirk and victory is essential. The Bairns and Rangers have been really consistent. While Hibs were overcoming Dumbarton, Rangers were being held at home by Queen of the South with just minutes remaining to play. They were then awarded their obligatory penalty, which they proceeded to miss. Any hopes Hibs had of reducing Rangers' lead in the title race by two points were dashed unfortunately when Martyn Waghorn scored in the ninety-fifth minute to maintain the Gers' 100% league record.

Hibs have ground out a 1–0 win at Falkirk courtesy of a Jason Cummings penalty. Referee Alan Muir gave the award after a collision between John McGinn and Falkirk's Blair Alston and it was pretty soft. Mind you, Hibs get so many stonewall penalty claims turned down that it was nice for them to get the benefit of the (not insignificant) doubt for once. This was Hibs' third penalty of the season. Both Hearts and Rangers are approaching double figures in the spot kick department so Hibs have a bit to go before catching them up.

The hard-fought and vital three points won at the Westfield Stadium certainly help Hibs in their quest to make up ground on Rangers at the top of the Championship table. There is now an eight-point gap between the sides so Hibs must win their next match at Stark's Park. Raith Rovers have won their last five league matches so a very difficult game is in prospect.

Falkirk certainly proved tough to beat. They were cheered on by a larger-than-usual, noisy crowd and the AstroTurf playing surface was as tricky as ever. Falkirk employed long balls in to the box and attempted to capitalise on long throws. Fortunately, Hibs didn't go back up the M9 with long faces.

Alan Stubbs couldn't resist a little dig at his opposite number Peter Houston at full time. In his post-match interview, Stubbs harked back to Houston's comments after last season's Scottish Cup semi-final about Hibs' inability to defend crosses. He reminded his rival that this time Hibs had managed to defend every cross that came into their box. Houston, for his part, declared that he felt that there was very little between the teams, given the disparity in resources in Hibs' favour between the two clubs. He had a point.

With the mission to gain three points at Falkirk duly accomplished, thoughts now turn to an equally crucial encounter in Kirkcaldy. Raith Rovers are having a great season under their impressive new manager Ray McKinnon. They are unbeaten at home and, as always, will present a difficult challenge.

In Jon Daly they have a centre-forward with physical attributes, aerial prowess and a lot of footballing nous. He will definitely bear watching. Former Hibee Scott Robertson is now also on Raith's books. Robbo is an excellent player and will have a point to prove to the manager who didn't retain his services.

Much has been made in the media this week about the strength of Hibs squad and the strength of the group is undeniable. Alan Pattulo in the *Scotsman* quoted the old footballing truism about the strength of a team being judged by the strength of its bench. Hibs most certainly have strength in depth. That will count for nothing if they don't win games like the encounter with Raith.

Hibs beat Raith Rovers 2–1 at Stark's Park. A dominant first half, which brought about a 2–0 interval lead that could and should have been more, was followed by a predictable second-half struggle. As expected, Jon Daly was a handful and he pulled a goal back for Raith in the sixty-fourth minute. For the rest of the match Raith pressed for an equaliser and Hibs were forced to defend. Hibs' own website used the word 'bombarded' to describe the pressure which Rovers applied to the Hibs goal. Thankfully the team held out to secure a highly important three points.

It's great to win but I cannot be alone in thinking that Hibs should be winning games like this more comfortably after enjoying such first-half dominance. The team seems to persist in making things hard for itself and its supporters (2,000 of whom travelled to Kirkcaldy).

On the positive side, Hibs have significantly more points than

The 1902 Hibernian team group shows off an impressive array of trophies.
One of them would prove rather difficult to win again in future.

Darren McGregor gives Hibs the lead against Raith Rovers and,
in the process, scores the club's 1000th Scottish Cup goal.

The late late show: Paul Hanlon manages to squeeze home Hibs' last-minute equaliser in the fifth-round match against Hearts at Tynecastle.

Stokes at the double: The Hibs striker fires home his second goal in the quarter-final replay against Inverness Caledonian Thistle.

Penalty shoot-out hero Conrad Logan dives to his right to push away Billy McKay's semi-final spot kick.

'Stokesy on Fire': Hibs have the early lead in the Scottish Cup final and Anthony Stokes celebrates his precision strike.

The vital equaliser: Anthony Stokes eludes his marker and heads Hibs level in the final against Rangers.

The goal that made history: David Gray bullets home his iconic Scottish Cup winning header.

'Some people are on the pitch…': Hibs fans run on to the field in celebration when the final whistle blows.

The Scottish Cup has been presented and it's time to head for home. The Bracks are one very happy family.

Scenes of joy as Hibs' open-top bus reaches the Foot of the Walk.

Bringing home the Holy Grail. Captain David Gray and Manager Alan Stubbs carry the Scottish Cup into Easter Road on their return from Hampden.

Sunshine on Leith Links on the day of the victory parade.

they had at the same stage last season and have now closed to within five points of Rangers.

Just like Hearts last year, Rangers have made an unbelievably consistent start to the season. Who would have expected them to still have a 100% record at the end of October? They are also similar to last season's Hearts team in that they manage to grind out wins even in games which prove difficult for them which is, I suppose, what Hibs have done at Falkirk and Raith in the last few days. Even if Rangers keep winning, they are about to visit Easter Road, which will provide Hibs with a great opportunity to reduce Rangers' lead at the top of the Championship.

Rangers have seen off St Mirren 1–0 in Paisley to keep their run going but the Buddies made them fight all the way. The Gers are once again eight points ahead of Hibs. Looking at Rangers' line up, with the exception of the prolific and powerful James Tavernier at right-back, the confident and determined Lee Wallace at left-back and the predatory Martyn Waghorn up front, Hibs have little to fear. The game against Rangers at the beginning of next month is shaping up to be a pivotal day in the race for promotion. Can Hibs be good enough and strong enough to prevail? We will know soon enough.

It is now twenty-four years since Hibs' 'Team that Wouldn't Die' beat Dunfermline 2–0 in the 1991 Skol Cup Final at Hampden. What a day that was. Hibs, in sight of a major trophy, a little over a year after escaping the predatory clutches of Wallace Mercer and his hostile takeover bid, allowed tension to get the better of them in a closely contested first half. At half time Alex Miller famously told his team that if they didn't win this match, they would 'regret it until the day they died'. He couldn't have said anything more concisely motivating, and goals from a Tommy McIntyre penalty and Keith Wright (who scored in every round of the competition) were enough to secure a famous victory.

Both goals meant something to the Brack family. My youngest son Kevin who was only six at the time (he is now a thirty-one-year-old headteacher) won £17 on the supporters' bus sweepstake as he had drawn big Tommy to score the first goal and Keith had played for me with distinction when I managed the Edinburgh Primary Schools football team. Among other schoolboy achievements, he scored a hat-trick against Dundee Schools at Tannadice in the first leg of the 1977 Scottish Cup Final. Edinburgh won that game 5–1 and secured the trophy 8–2 on aggregate.

Hibs showed the goals on their own TV channel this week. Watching them again answered a couple of questions that have exercised my memory. Was the penalty award for the first goal correct? Well, yes, it was as Raymond Sharp grabbed hold of Mickey Weir causing him to lose his balance. It was a fairly soft award though. Then again, was Keith Wright offside when he clinched the game for Hibs? It was a close call but, no, he wasn't. He was actually played onside by none other than Davie Moyes in the centre of the Dunfermline defence.

What a night followed that game. Incredible crowds turned out to welcome the team home and all the emotion built up by Mercer's attempt to finish off the Hibs poured out onto the streets of Edinburgh in a giant celebration of a very special occasion.

As if that wasn't enough, when the team eventually reached Easter Road, the old ground was full and this inspired some of the players so much that they serenaded the fans with their version of 'Glory Glory to the Hibees'. Happy memories indeed. Whether there will be similar celebrations at the end of season 2015–16 remains to be seen but hope springs eternal.

November 2015

The Winning Run Continues

Victory over Rangers – Dundee United blown away in League Cup – monthly awards for Stubbs and Cummings – the victories keep on coming

Hibs have beaten Rangers 2–1 and what a game it was! Jason Cummings scored a brilliant goal early on and then Dylan McGeouch, who had started the game superbly, had to go off injured.

Hibs got to half time relatively comfortably but Rangers equalised early in the second half when a Lee Wallace shot was deflected past Mark Oxley by Darren McGregor. Jason Cummings should have put Hibs ahead again when he showed terrific control and great pace to latch on to a wonder pass from John McGinn and outstrip the Rangers defence. Unfortunately, he shot straight at Wes Foderingham in the Rangers goal.

Rangers then hit the bar before Paul Hanlon headed home a John McGinn corner. Rangers hit the woodwork once more but

Hibs held on for a crucial win which brings them once again to within five points of Rangers so maybe the race for automatic promotion is not over after all. Man of the match was undoubtedly the tireless McGinn who combines non-stop energy with a large measure of skill. He has been a tremendous signing.

Jason Cummings was again razor sharp and he just keeps on improving. Lewis Stevenson was as committed as ever at the back, both centre halves did well and Dominique Malonga started the game really well but lost his way as the match progressed. Goalkeeper Mark Oxley put in a very impressive performance.

After the game, Alan Stubbs admitted that, despite his pre-match claims to the contrary, Hibs would have really struggled to win the Championship title if they had lost this match. Thankfully they didn't. Stubbs also praised the support given to their team by the Hibs fans which was good to hear. He followed this up by appealing to these Hibs followers who have lost the habit of going to Easter Road to return to the fold. I hope there is a positive response to that request.

Rangers boss Mark Warburton said that his dressing room was full of very angry players because his team had lost a match he and they thought that they deserved to win. Rangers had pace and were slick in possession and didn't enjoy too much luck apart from their deflected goal but they had no real reason to feel hard done by.

Hibs now have two tough games in the next six days. They face Dundee United in the League Cup quarter-final at Easter Road in midweek and make the journey to Paisley to play St Mirren in the Championship three days later (arguably a more important game). The players put in a gargantuan effort against Rangers and there will undoubtedly be tired legs in the squad. I think that it is really important that Alan Stubbs takes advantage of the fresher legs in his playing group in midweek and utilises all the options available to him.

James Keatings, Fraser Fyvie, Liam Fontaine, Adam Eckersley, Islam Feruz and Danny Carmichael, who have had less game time than those who play week in and week out, should all feature in my view. Hopefully Dylan McGeouch's injury will not be too serious as he is a fine player. He definitely suffers his fair share of injuries though.

Quite a few people have had something to say about Hibs' victory over Rangers. Former Hibee Michael O'Neill who has done a brilliant job in steering Northern Ireland to the finals of the European Championships was at the game.

He declared afterwards that anything other than a win would have made it impossible for Hibs to gain automatic promotion. He added that yesterday's result has now given Hibs a realistic chance of winning the title. He is right on both counts.

Jason Cummings was as irrepressible as ever. He said that his strike yesterday was his 'best goal ever'. He also said that he didn't see Hibs losing any time soon. That prediction might fall by the wayside sooner than he thinks. Cummings ended by stating that the pressure was now on Rangers and expressed doubt as to whether they would be able to cope with it. Jason is not a man who is destined for a career in the diplomatic service.

Leigh Griffiths, who is having a magnificent season with Celtic and demonstrating to the football world just how good a player he is (everyone with a Hibs connection knew his worth already), took Cummings to task last season for his claim after scoring at Ibrox that he had 'a touch like an angel'. Leigh called Jason a

'Billy Big Time' on that occasion. This time round he has only had praise for the man who has succeeded him as Hibs' number one striker, which is as it should be. Just imagine Griffiths and Cummings playing up front together for Hibs. They would be unstoppable.

There has been some very interesting material on the managerial front. Michael O'Neill was interviewed at length on BBC Scotland and disclosed that he was very close to being appointed manager of Hibs in 2011 when Pat Fenlon was given the job. O'Neill met with two Easter Road directors for five hours, felt that the meeting had gone really well and then never heard another word. Kenny MacIntyre, hosting the programme, suggested that this may have been because of malicious rumours doing the rounds at the time that O'Neill had a drink problem. Michael conceded that there may be some truth in this theory but emphatically denied having any problems with alcohol.

Hibs certainly missed a trick in not going for O'Neill and it was discourteous of them not to get back to him after his interview. I doubt that we would be where we are now if Michael O'Neill had been in charge rather than Pat Fenlon and then Terry Butcher. It was a very honest and revealing interview and all credit to the Northern Ireland boss for opening up the way he did. O'Neill was a superb player for Hibs. He was highly skilled, had great vision and scored his fair share of goals. He is proving to be pretty talented as a manager too.

Alan Stubbs has also been very frank. He has stated that if he had known how bad a state Hibs were in when he took over as manager, he wouldn't have accepted the job in the first place. Personally I find that remark disappointing as I would have hoped that Stubbs would have relished the opportunity to turn round such a big club as Hibs irrespective of the state he found them in. That said he is doing a really good job and a big part of that has been his ability to identify and sign good players. Another thing Stubbs has said is that managers 'live or die by their recruitment.' He is absolutely right.

His three predecessors – Colin Calderwood, Pat Fenlon and Terry Butcher – all performed very poorly in the recruitment department. When thinking of their signings, names like Matt Thornhill, Fraser Mullen, Rowan Vine and Danny Haynes spring to mind. No more needs to be said.

Former Hibs manager Mixu Paatelainen will bring his Dundee United team to Easter Road for the League Cup quarter-final after they managed to win their first game under him against Ross County at the weekend.

Like a lot of Hibs fans, I have a great deal of affection for Mixu who served Hibs admirably as a player and was improving as a manager when he left suddenly only eighteen months into his reign. Alan Stubbs played with the big man at Bolton and has spoken highly of him in the build up to the game.

Finally on the managerial front, Alex Miller, who managed Hibs for ten years between 1986 and 1996 and won the Skol Cup with the club in 1991, has been appointed to a coaching position assisting Ian Murray at St Mirren at the age of sixty-six. So when Hibs travel to Paisley after facing two tough games against Rangers and Dundee United in the space of three days, their former manager and ex-captain will be lying in wait for them. An extremely tricky assignment is in prospect.

Hibs completely outplayed Dundee United and beat them 3–0. It was the most convincing and one-sided Hibs victory I can remember for a very long time. Dundee United, clearly low in confidence after their struggles in the Premier League were simply blown away. Hibs really could have scored six or seven goals such was their dominance. Their high-energy performance was all the more impressive coming, as it did, only three days after the win over Rangers. Hibs have now beaten two Premiership clubs in the League Cup and are undoubtedly good enough to go up.

Alan Stubbs described the past few days as the best of his time at Hibs and he has been rewarded for his team's recent excellent form by being given the Manager of the Month award for October. Unfortunately our manager's first-class work is continuing to attract attention from elsewhere. Queen's Park Rangers have just sacked their manager Chris Ramsey and are being credited with interest not only in Stubbs but in Rangers boss Mark Warburton. Wouldn't it be good if they went for 'Warbo'. In the words of Kevin Keegan, I would 'love it, absolutely love it.'

Jason Cummings has been named as October's Player of the Month and he thoroughly deserves it. He has scored in his last six matches and has played really well in all of them too. His all-round game is also really improving. Interviewed on STV yesterday, Jason was asked to tell the viewers about 'the real Jason Cummings'. He replied, in typically irrepressible style, 'What is this – a dating website?'

David Gray and Lewis Stevenson joined Cummings on the scoresheet against United. Someone else who should have scored was Farid El Alagui who tasted first-team action for the first time this season when he came on as a late substitute. Martin Boyle, also on as a sub, laid on an absolute sitter for Farid but, from point blank range, he completely missed his kick. Still it was good to see him back.

Now, a very tired Hibs side will have to gird their loins once again and go and win in Paisley in three days' time. A defeat or draw against St Mirren would undo all the previous good work. It won't be easy because even the indefatigable John McGinn went off with fatigue last night. Let's hope that Hibs can raise themselves one more time and see off Ian Murray, Alex Miller and their Saints.

The half-time draw in the Dundee United match was made by Derek Riordan. It was good to see him back on the Easter Road pitch and he received a good reception. He is still training at East Mains and it's not out of the question that he could sign for Hibs for a third time.

Riordan's old strike partner, Garry O'Connor, is now manager of Selkirk in the East of Scotland League on a permanent basis. He earned his elevation from 'acting' to 'permanent' after losing his first match in charge 5–1, which is an interesting way to make an appointment. Big Garry has already declared that he wants to manage Hibs one day. If that ever comes to pass, I would love to be a fly on the wall in the East Mains dressing room when Mr O'Connor lectures his players on the values of living a disciplined lifestyle.

Hibs have beaten St Mirren 4–1 to cap a highly impressive six days of football. They didn't start well, mind you. St Mirren went ahead after only eight minutes after Hibs switched off when defending a corner. Hibs defending has definitely been better of late but here they were again conceding a very avoidable goal. On this occasion though it did no harm. Within two minutes, Jason Cummings had equalised with a slide rule finish and after that, it was the James Keatings show.

First Keats ran onto an excellent free kick from Liam Henderson to fire the ball across Jamie Langfield. He then came up with an exquisite curled finish into the top right-hand corner of the net to send Hibs in 3–1 up at half time. When Liam Henderson was brought down in the box in the second half, Jason Cummings had been substituted. There was only one man to take the penalty in most people's eyes and that, of course, was Keatings who was on a hat-trick. Dominique Malonga had other ideas though and attempted to take the ball and the kick but captain David Gray soon disabused him of that notion and handed the ball to Keatings, who made no mistake as he sent Langfield the wrong way from the spot.

This was an important win for Hibs and it was just as well that they did dig deep to overcome tiredness and secure three points because Falkirk beat Raith away and Rangers also won again. Falkirk rarely lose. Peter Houston has created a strong-minded ultra-competitive team who should not be underestimated.

As for Rangers, they comfortably disposed of Alloa at Ibrox to the tune of 4–0. After the game, their striker Martyn Waghorn who now has seventeen goals this season declared that he wasn't at all worried about Hibs as Rangers were better than them. He's clearly no shrinking violet, Mr Waghorn, as he also stated that he expects to score thirty goals before the end of the season. We shall see on both counts.

As for Hibs, they go into the latest international break in great shape and good heart. Next weekend Jason Cummings, John McGinn and Liam Henderson will represent Scotland Under 21s against Ukraine. Henderson played particularly well at Paisley being involved in three of Hibs' four goals. He has said that it would mean a lot to him to help Hibs to win the Championship. He stated that, in his opinion, Hibs are far too big a club to be in the second tier of Scottish football. He is absolutely right.

One man who didn't cover himself in glory in the St Mirren match was Dominique Malonga, who behaved in a very petulant fashion when he didn't get to take Hibs' penalty. His attitude did him no favours and he has to realise it's about the team not just about himself. He is an extremely talented player with bags of skill and the ability to score outstanding goals. He is definitely somewhat enigmatic though.

In their last seven games, Hibs have won away at Queen of the South, Falkirk, Raith Rovers and St Mirren and recorded home victories over Dumbarton, Rangers and Dundee United – a truly outstanding effort. Great praise is due to Alan Stubbs and his players. Now they have to keep up the good work.

Hibs have been drawn against St Johnstone in the League Cup semi-final. The Saints have been flying under Tommy Wright, but it's a decent draw and certainly better than a tie with Celtic who will play Ross County in the other semi-final. The game will be played at the end of January 2016 and I hope that the SPFL play the match at Tynecastle. This would suit both sets of fans and ensure a full house and tremendous atmosphere.

The last time Hibs played St Johnstone in the League Cup was the semi-final in Gorgie in 2007. Saints were in the old First Division at the time and managed by Owen Coyle. They gave Hibs a really tough match. Steven Fletcher put Hibs in front but the Saints equalised and Hibs were relieved to take the game into extra time after surviving a number of defensive scares. Hibs pulled away in the extra half hour though and a David Murphy free kick and a clever solo goal from Benji took them to Hampden and glory in the shape of a 5–1 win over Kilmarnock. The fact that Killie were under the control of Jim Jefferies and Billy Brown made that victory all the sweeter.

There has been a mutual admiration society in operation at Easter Road recently. Jason Cummings set the ball rolling when he said how much he was enjoying training alongside Derek

Riordan and how Riordan was helping him to be a better player and to score more goals, which was good to hear.

Next came Farid El Alagui who claimed that he was at last fully fit and ready to return to first-team action. He joined in the praise game by saying how well his fellow strikers at Hibs were doing and making it clear that he realised that he would have to fight for his place. That was also good to hear.

Finally we had John McGinn extolling the virtues of Alan Stubbs. According to John, he had to choose from several clubs when making his decision on his next career move last summer. He now knows that Alan Stubbs was the right manager for him and that Hibs was definitely the best club he could have signed for. That's even better to hear.

Scotland Under 21s, captained by John McGinn, have drawn 2–2 with Ukraine. McGinn and Jason Cummings, who scored one and created the other of Scotland's goals, were very impressive. Liam Henderson had a quieter game.

There is still a lot of complimentary comment being shared around at Easter Road. Alan Stubbs has sung the praises of Paul Hanlon. Paul, now twenty-five, has reached the milestone of playing 250 games for Hibs. His manager just sees him getting better and better as his experience continues to grow. I would have to agree. Paul is out of contract at the end of the season and the sooner Hibs get his signature on a new deal, the better.

Falkirk, in action because the international break doesn't affect them, have beaten Alloa 5–0 and closed to within a point of Hibs. The Bairns are really flying this season and are a definite threat to both Rangers and Hibs.

Adam Eckersley who is yet to play a first-team game for Hibs has declared himself bemused by Hearts' decision to let him go at the end of last season. He claims that crossing the divide to Hibs has not caused him any major difficulties but seems more intent on looking back on his time at Tynecastle than on focusing on what the future might hold for him at Easter Road.

He did say that he would be prepared to consider extending his contract with Hibs when his current deal runs out in January, which is a change from his previous position when he seemed dead set on going to America at that point. Eckersley is a fast, powerful player who enhances Hibs' squad but his priority now has to be getting himself some game time, proving that he has recovered from the knee injury which has kept him out since the end of last season and showing that he can still play to the level he displayed for Hearts last season.

Brighton, who are currently topping the English Championship have joined Bournemouth, Cardiff, Fulham and Rotherham in showing an interest in signing Jason Cummings. If I was Alan Stubbs, I would only have one message for these clubs and that message would be 'Hands off Jason Cummings. He's a Hibs player and he is staying a Hibs player.'

Hibs are about to return to Championship action with a midweek home game against Livingston. As ever in this ultra-tight league, a victory is essential. Three points would help Hibs close to within two points of Rangers, albeit with one more game played. Livingston won't make it easy, that's for sure, and Hibs will need to be at their best.

Two weeks ago, Alan Stubbs spoke about Rangers having a budget four times the size of that of Hibs. Rangers manager Mark Warburton has responded to those comments. He accused Stubbs of pulling figures 'out of the sky' and advised him to concentrate on his own team.

For his part, Stubbs has kept a low profile putting his first-team coach John Doolan forward for the Livingston pre-match interviews. I thought that Doolan spoke very impressively. He showed a true commitment to Hibs cause and clearly values being part of a great club and realises the huge potential at Easter Road.

One comment made by Doolan, though, might not go down too well with his boss. Referring to the ongoing war of words between Stubbs and Mark Warburton, he compared them, in a throwaway line, to television's Chuckle Brothers, a children's comedy duo who spend a lot of time bickering good-naturedly with each other.

Hibs beat Livingston 2–1 to cut Rangers lead at the top of the Championship to two points. On a miserable, wet, windy night, the atmosphere was subdued and this may have affected Hibs' performance.

Dominique Malonga was away on international duty with Congo (he has been an unused substitute in both of his country's games so his lengthy journey has been a bit of a waste of time) and was replaced by Martin Boyle. Darren McGregor came back into the team in place of Paul Hanlon who missed out through a hamstring injury.

Livingston were organised and resolute but Hibs should have won much more comfortably than they did. As is often the case, a host of really good chances were spurned. On this occasion, Jason Cummings was the worst offender. He could have had a hat-trick and was guilty of one particularly glaring miss when he rounded the goalkeeper and, with the empty goal in front of him, hit the ball into the side net. John McGinn and Fraser Fyvie also missed excellent opportunities but thankfully James Keatings had his shooting boots on.

Keats struck two excellent left-foot shots to give Hibs a 2–0 lead. John McGinn provided a brilliant assist for the first of these counters but the second strike was all Keatings' own work. Indeed he came very close to notching his second successive hat-trick when he just missed the target with an acrobatic overhead kick.

Just when Hibs should have been in cruise control, they switched off in the eighty-sixth minute to allow Jordan Sheerin to pull back a goal for Livingston and the last few minutes ended up being far more nerve-wracking than they should have been. Hibs were actually reduced to holding the ball at the corner flag to run down the clock. The team has to cut out its costly habit of conceding unnecessary and avoidable goals.

Defensively it was not an impressive performance. Both Liam Fontaine and Darren McGregor were below their best, Mark Oxley twice punched the ball when he should have caught it and Lewis Stevenson gave the ball away carelessly in the lead up to Livingston's goal.

Further forward, Martin Boyle was totally ineffective. He is always better when he comes on as a substitute and is able to run at tiring defences. Islam Feruz made a rare appearance when he came on for Jason Cummings who was uncharacteristically out of sorts. Feruz did nothing and it is fair to say that since joining up at Easter Road at the end of August, he has shown very little of the talent that he is supposed to have.

Alan Stubbs made pointed reference to John Doolan's 'Chuckle Brothers' comments when he said, 'if you put your assistant up to speak, there can be a few headlines, but I don't intend to be part of the pantomime season.' Stubbs has had the last laugh, though, as Hibs have picked up three very valuable points. Mark Warburton and his assistant David Weir left Easter Road early and I am sure that Warburton wouldn't have been chuckling.

The crowd on a very inclement evening was just under 8,000. I am sure that, if this game had been played on Saturday afternoon as it should have been, there would have been more than 10,000 there. It is a bit much that clubs battling for promotion have to inconvenience themselves and their supporters by being forced to rearrange vital matches due to their players' involvement in international Under 21 fixtures. Having to reschedule this game cost Hibs money and disrupted their momentum. I don't know if many people care passionately about Scotland Under 21 games or not. My only interest in these affairs is that the Hibs players return injury-free.

As I suspected would be the case, Alan Stubbs wasn't best pleased with John Doolan referring to Mark Warburton and himself as the Chuckles Brothers. Interviewed on STV, he did his best to make light of a question which homed in on Doolan's remarks, saying, 'Well, we're all in the entertainment business, aren't we?' He did make it clear, however, that his assistant would not be making any further media appearances in the near future.

Hibs announced today that Eddie Turnbull, a great for the club both as a player and a manager, has been posthumously awarded the Arctic Star decoration for his service in the Arctic convoys during the Second World War. A brave man, both on and off the football field.

Hibs travel next to Clackmannanshire to meet Alloa at the Indrodill Stadium, a ground which used to be known as

Recreation Park. Alloa's abode may have a more grandiose name but it also has one of the worst playing surfaces in Scotland. The AstroTurf there has a very thin top layer making the pitch hard underfoot and difficult to play on. Having now closed to within two points of Rangers, yet again Hibs cannot afford any slip-ups. Here's hoping the winning streak continues.

The French national anthem 'La Marseillaise' will be played at all English and Scottish Premier League grounds this weekend as a mark of respect after last week's terrorist atrocities in Paris. It is a particularly stirring anthem. When Hibs played it before a match at Easter Road against St Mirren as Franck Sauzée led the team out during his time as captain it had a real impact on the emotions. I am sure the renditions across the country will touch the hearts and minds of everyone present at all the games.

On BBC's *Football Focus*, there was a feature on Derek Adams. Adams is now in charge of Plymouth Argyle and doing really well. Argyle are five points in front at the top of League 2. He also had a really impressive CV when he was manager of Ross County. Yet his short-lived spell as number 2 to Colin Calderwood was singularly unsuccessful. I suspect that this had more to do with Calderwood than with Adams. Of all Hibs' unsuccessful managerial appointments in recent years, Calderwood was, in my opinion, undoubtedly the worst. Maybe if Rod Petrie had made Derek Adams manager rather than assistant manager, things might have turned out differently.

Well Hibs did it but only just! They beat Alloa 1–0 at the Indodrill thanks to a fine Jason Cummings finish after he was put through on goal by a superb pass from John McGinn. In truth, Hibs should have won far more comfortably than they did but they are now level on points with Rangers who were held to a draw by Livingston at Almondvale. That result didn't surprise me as Livi were very resilient indeed when they were at Easter Road.

It was quite an interesting day on the former Hibs goalkeepers' front. Andy McNeil, who kept goal for Hibs in the 5–1 League Cup final win over Kilmarnock in 2007, was in goal for Alloa but had to retire at half time with a back injury. Graeme Smith, who was signed for Hibs as part of John Hughes' 'goalkeeping school' along with Graeme Stack and Mark Brown, is now at Brechin and turned up for their match against Stenhousemuir yesterday at the wrong ground. Having arrived incorrectly at Ochilview, Smith then covered the eighty-seven miles to Glebe Park in time for kick-off. His team still lost though.

Alan Stubbs has given his players a well-deserved few days break as Hibs don't play again until December when they travel to Cappielow to meet Morton. I hope that Stubbs takes a few days off himself. He certainly deserves it as he has done brilliantly so far this season.

There is news today that Liam Henderson who missed the game at Alloa is suffering from an unidentified viral infection. Alan Stubbs has sent Henderson for blood tests and says that the youngster is feeling 'wiped out'. This is a real shame for Henderson and goes some way towards explaining why he seems to tire in some games. He clearly is a talented player with bags of skill, the ability to whip in dangerous balls from set pieces and a willingness to give his all for the cause. Let's hope that the medical people can find out what's causing the problem and treat it successfully. Hibs need all their best players fit, and to have 'Hendo' firing on all cylinders once again can only be a good thing.

Hibs have announced a revamp of their scouting system. Graeme Mathie, Head of Player Recruitment, has taken on a number of extra scouts in the hope that Hibs will be able to identify and sign more of the best young players in Scotland. As a team renowned for its youth development, this is exactly what Hibs should be doing. It would be great if the reorganised scouting structure paid dividends.

Hibs still have a few injured players who are short of game time. One man who most definitely does not come into the category is John McGinn who has been an ever present since coming on as a substitute in the second half of Hibs' first league game of the season at Dumbarton. He has also captained Scotland Under 21s on four occasions.

Alan Stubbs has said that he had wanted to give McGinn a break for a few weeks now. However, he has been such an influential player in almost every match that Stubbs couldn't afford to leave him out. Like the rest of Hibs' first-team regulars, McGinn is currently enjoying a few days off. In his case, the break is richly deserved and will hopefully recharge his batteries for the restart of league fixtures at Cappielow against Morton on the first Saturday in December.

I have just celebrated my sixth-eighth birthday and it has coincided with two landmark occasions on the sporting front for Great Britain. Tyson Fury has defeated Wladimir Klitscho to become World Heavy Weight Boxing Champion and Andy Murray, playing tennis of an unbelievably high standard, has inspired Great Britain to its first Davis Cup win since 1936.

Hibs have had a quiet week with most of the first-team squad receiving an extended break from Alan Stubbs. During their time off, they have had two pats on the back from two famous Hibee Pats. Pat Stanton feels that Hibs are a much more resilient side now and much less likely to crumble under pressure.

Pat McGinlay sees similarities to the Championship-winning team which he played in and thinks that Hibs can win the league. I very much hope that they are both right.

I have just received my first ever Hibernian shareholders' report and my invitation to the club's AGM which will be held on 15 December. The headline statistic was the fact that Hibs lost £840,000 during their first year in the Championship. The report was accompanied by a letter from Rod Petrie. Mr Petrie explained last season's deficit by the fact that Hibs had continued to operate as a Premiership club while competing in Scottish football's second tier.

That makes sense but it is vital that Hibs get promotion this season. Whether it is by winning the league or through the play-offs, they just have to come up. We neither need nor want another season doing battle with the Dumbartons and the Alloas. Hibs are not in a bad situation financially after the restructuring of their debt. Twenty per cent of the club is now owned by supporters which is great. It is clear though Hibs cannot continue to function at their current level while drawing home crowds of around 8,000–9,000. They must get back to where they belong in the Premiership with its increased gate revenue.

A lot of the report's financial information was fairly impenetrable to the lay person but you have to trust those in charge of the club when they tell us that we are in a relatively healthy state. I am looking forward to the AGM, which hopefully will be both interesting and informative.

On a lighter note (much lighter!), Hibs playing squad completed their week off from training and playing by taking part in their annual Christmas night out at the weekend. It was a fancy dress affair and some of the players' choice of costumes was interesting to say the least. Paul Hanlon went as Pinocchio, complete with a false, long nose, and Martin Boyle went as Tinkerbell the Fairy. Unsurprisingly, Jason Cummings surpassed the rest of his teammates when he turned up dressed as Little Bo Peep. To add authenticity to his performance, he was carrying an artificial sheep. These are supposed to be grown men with intellects to match. Ah well, I suppose it was just a bit of harmless fun. Let's hope that Bo Peep will be back on the goal trail when the action restarts.

December 2015

Defeat at Ibrox

Scottish Cup draw – Falkirk stalemate – late, late show against Queens – setback at Ibrox

The draw for the fourth round of the Scottish Cup, which takes place early next year, was made today. Hibs came out of the hat with an away match against Raith Rovers. Alan Stubbs made it clear that he considers the tie a tricky proposition and he is right. He also feels that Hibs' next league match at Morton will be extremely tough. Morton are fourth in the Championship and on an unbeaten run. They will be difficult to beat.

The prospect of the Scottish Cup is a very alluring one. Hibs came close last year when they lost really unluckily to Falkirk in the semi-final. They have come close many times before of course and ultimately fallen short. When the Scottish Cup final comes round in May 2016, it will be 114 years since Hibs last collected world football's oldest trophy. Mind you, the team which has beaten Raith Rovers in recent seasons, has gone on to win the cup. Could that be an omen?

Leeann Dempster made it clear that Hibs are not at all keen to sell any players when the transfer window opens in January. She says that they are more interested in bringing new players in. That is good to hear.

Derek Collins, who was Hibs' right-back under Alex McLeish in the team of Franck Sauzée and Russell Latapy, has been looking ahead to Hibs' upcoming match with Morton. Collins, of course, spent the majority of his career at Cappielow so he knows both teams well. He was very complimentary about Hibs and made it clear that he considered them to be a major football club. Collins will be best remembered, of course, for scoring the winning goal against Falkirk in the pivotal promotion match at Brockville in 1999 which also happened to be Franck Sauzée's debut for Hibs. He thinks it will be close when his two old teams meet but expects Hibs to 'edge it'.

Jamie Montgomery, the Hibs supporter who produces a weekly column for the *Daily Record*, has written today of how he is finding this season to be extremely stressful with every weekend throwing up a 'must-win' game. I am glad someone else feels the same way as me. So many of the Championship teams are capable of causing an upset that every match, especially the away ones, is a potential banana skin.

Hibs just cannot afford to drop points as Rangers, who have recorded two consecutive 4–0 victories since drawing with Livingston, just don't seem likely to slip up very often. Fulham are keen to make Mark Warburton their new manager but unfortunately it looks like he is going to stay at Ibrox.

Hibs' match away to Morton has been called off. The pitch was playable but travelling conditions weren't safe. That is not surprising as the weather has been absolutely foul with a mixture of driving rain and gale force winds wreaking havoc as Storm Desmond has battered the country. The conditions wouldn't have suited Hibs' style of play but it means that when they meet Falkirk at Easter Road in their next game, it will be their first game for three weeks which is far from ideal. Falkirk and Rangers have also had their games postponed so at least Hibs didn't lose any ground in the race for the Championship.

Alan Stubbs and John McGinn have been named as Manager of the Month and Player of the Month for November. Both accolades were richly deserved and Stubbs also won the award in October. He has been linked with the vacant manager's position at English Championship team Reading. This is the latest in a series of jobs down South for which Hibs boss has been 'mentioned in dispatches'. Stubbs says that he cannot control speculation and is only focused on his job at Easter Road. Hibs fans would certainly miss him if he left. He has brought an air of positivity back to Hibs and has proved that he has an excellent eye for a player.

A fourteen-year-old Hibs supporter, Brandon Walker, has passed away. John McGinn visited the lad in hospital only last week. McGinn and Alan Stubbs will attend Brandon's funeral and the fans will applaud him in the fourteenth minute of the vital game against Falkirk at the weekend which is a nice tribute for a young Hibee whose life has ended far, far too soon. Stubbs dedicated his Manager of the Month award to Brandon too, which was a thoughtful gesture.

I went along to an event at the Hibs' Supporters Club with my son Dominic and my daughter Lisa. St Patrick's Branch was hosting a question-and-answer session with Alan Stubbs, John

Doolan and George Craig – Hibs' Head of Football Operations. St Pat's is an excellent, proactive branch which has lots of innovative ideas and does a lot of good.

It was a very enjoyable night and all three club representatives performed impressively. Stubbs was commendably honest and you could tell from listening to him why he has done so well. Like all top managers, and I think that is exactly what he will become in time, he has an aura of command about him and you can see why his players respond to him.

Three of his answers were quite significant. He made it clear that he would not be offering Derek Riordan a contract, which is a shame. He stated that any remarks he makes about Rangers will be accurate and factual so that no one at Ibrox or in the media can have any complaints about them. He claimed that he had Rangers rattled and intended to keep on rattling them. Stubbs also said that he was a believer in fate and that he felt that it was fate that had brought him to Easter Road for his first managerial post as he had made his comeback from a life-threatening illness there as a Celtic player and been given a reception from the Hibs support, which will always live with him.

The one answer Alan gave which I didn't agree with was when someone asked him if he would like to see Hibs scoring more goals and winning games more convincingly. He replied that he was quite happy to win by one goal. If you are one goal up in the final minutes, you are always vulnerable to a late equaliser and the unnecessary loss of points. If you are well ahead, then you are comfortable. It is surely better to be comfortable.

It was a great session, though, and it is clear that, at present, Hibs are in good hands. At the start of the meeting, young Brandon Walker's cousin spoke very movingly about Brandon and his love for Hibs. The minute's applause for him at the Falkirk game will be very poignant indeed. The fund for Brandon's funeral has been increased by a number of generous donations.

Quite a game between Hibs and Falkirk at Easter Road. Hibs were without Marvin Bartley and Dylan McGeouch through injury while there was no place on the bench for Farid El Alagui who must be having yet more injury problems and Islam Feruz who, I suspect, is heading back to Chelsea having singularly failed to make any impact at all with Hibs.

As most games against Peter Houston's well-drilled, totally committed Falkirk side are, this match was tight and evenly contested until John McGinn got sent off in the forty-third minute. John cut into the Falkirk penalty area from the right and overran the ball. He lunged rashly to recover it and caught Mark Kerr on the shin. Kerr, it has to be said, did not underplay the effect of the tackle. Kevin Clancy, the referee, had no hesitation in showing McGinn a red card. It seemed harsh as the tackle, while reckless, contained no malice whatsoever.

After half time, Hibs left Jason Cummings up front on his own, allowed Falkirk to dominate possession and played on the counter attack. It was effective. Lone striker Cummings broke clear and was brought down in the area by David McCracken. Referee Clancy saw what appeared to be a clear penalty as a dive and showed Jason a yellow card.

Worse was to follow. Mark Oxley hadn't had a save to make but in the eighty-fourth minute he dropped a soft shot from Blair Alston and ex-Hearts man Lee Miller, on as a substitute, followed up to net the rebound. It was a real Oxley howler.

To Hibs' great credit, they didn't give up and even when Lewis Stevenson went off with a head knock reducing the team to nine men, they continued to pour forward. In the ninety-second minute, Jason Cummings got to the byline and sent the ball low across goal. Henri Anier, making his first appearance as a substitute after his loan move from Dundee United at the end of August, skilfully flicked the ball on and Martin Boyle, another sub, arrived at the back post to knock the ball home and give Hibs a draw which they richly deserved.

After the game, Alan Stubbs said that it was a draw that felt like a win. He was absolutely right. Stubbs also described the match as being a pivotal moment in the season. Again, he was on the mark with his comment. Rangers drew at home to Morton so despite finishing the match with nine players, Hibs managed to avoid losing any ground in the battle for the Championship.

The one negative was John McGinn's ordering off. It was a questionable decision, and one which might cost Hibs dearly. McGinn could get a two- or three-match ban and miss the crucial game against Rangers at Ibrox just after Christmas. That would be a real bonus for the Gers and a significant blow for Hibs. Alan Stubbs has decided to appeal John McGinn's red card. Let's hope that the appeal is successful.

I watched the highlights of the Hibs vs. Falkirk match on BBC last night and I have to say that my initial judgement of the second of the two key refereeing decisions probably owed a bit to partisanship and did Mr Clancy a disservice.

Jason Cummings did indeed appear to dive in the second half when most Hibs fans, myself included, thought it was a stonewall penalty. It was foolish by Jason as he had beaten his man and made space for a shot. I don't like seeing Hibs players going down too easily in the box when there is the chance to score a goal.

I have attended my first ever Hibernian AGM as a fully fledged shareholder of the club. The meeting was packed and there was, in contrast to recent seasons, a very positive and harmonious atmosphere.

The meeting itself was brief and formal but, at its conclusion, there were three separate presentations from Alan Stubbs, the supporters on the club's board and Leeann Dempster. All the presentations were interesting, informative and enjoyable.

Alan Stubbs pointed out that Hibs were thirteen points better off, had scored more goals, conceded fewer and kept more clean sheets that they had at the corresponding time last season. You can't argue with facts like that.

Stubbs also gave a reassurance on the fitness of Farid El Alagui and stated that the club did not need to agree to the sale of any of its players in the January transfer window and that he certainly had no intention of letting go any player he wanted to keep. Hopefully that means that Jason Cummings will be going nowhere when the transfer window reopens next month.

Dempster spoke with passion and clarity. She said that there was every chance that supporters would again be given the chance to buy shares in Hibs in the not-too-distant future and that the process would be made easier this time. She also made it clear that she was happy at Hibs and had no intention of going anywhere else anytime soon.

Away from the AGM, Alan Stubbs today urged Islam Feruz

to stay and fight for a first team place. It has been rumoured that Feruz will be going back to Chelsea in January. Stubbs also stated that Dylan McGeouch will be fit to play against Queen of the South on Saturday, which is very good news.

It has been announced that Willie Collum will join English referees Martin Atkinson and Mark Clattenberg in officiating at the finals of Euro 2016 next summer. I find this news to be very surprising indeed. Any time I have watched Collum referee, his performance has been anything but impressive and, to my mind, full of errors.

John McGinn has won his appeal against his red card in the Falkirk match. It has been turned into a yellow card which means he is free to face Queen of the South at the weekend and Rangers at the end of December, which is great news and a massive boost.

Ian Murray has resigned as manager of St Mirren, having done very poorly there after a bright start to his managerial career with Dumbarton. Another former Hibee, Russell Latapy, is being touted as a possible successor for Murray. That would certainly be an interesting appointment.

Jose Mourinho has been sacked as manager of Chelsea just seven months after winning the Premier League title for season 2014–15. If the media follow recent precedent, Alan Stubbs' name will be linked with the vacancy at Stamford Bridge tomorrow.

Brandon Walker's funeral has taken place. Hundreds attended and those present included John McGinn, Alan Stubbs and Paul Kane. May young Brandon, true Hibee that he was, rest in peace.

Alan Stubbs has hinted at an eye-catching capture in January saying that he may 'pull a rabbit out of the hat'. Let's hope that he does. The bigger the signing, the better.

Next up for Hibs is Queen of the South at Easter Road and just like every week in the ultra-competitive Championship it is a must win game. Hibs just have to make it happen.

Before Hibs played Queen of the South, Falkirk beat Rangers 2–1 in the lunchtime match. There were two talking points – Falkirk's excellence and Willie Collum's refereeing. Peter Houston may not be the most popular of people as far as Hibs fans are concerned as he is clearly no lover of the Hibees but he has done an amazing job at the Falkirk Stadium and his team – as well as being very much in the mix for promotion from the Championship – did Hibs a real favour by taking points off Rangers.

As for Collum, he gave Falkirk a penalty for an offence which clearly took place outside the box and then gave Rangers the softest of spot kicks (which Martyn Waghorn missed) in added on time. He is, in my opinion, a very poor referee and his appointment to the finals of Euro 2016 remains difficult to understand.

So, all Hibs needed to do was go out and beat Queen of the South at home to go into Christmas level on points with Rangers. Boy did they make hard work of things. Their passing was poor and their first touch was more often than not simply not good enough. Fraser Fyvie and James Keatings were below their best and Jason Cummings and Martin Boyle who played up front made little impression.

Alan Stubbs took off his front two and replaced them with Henri Anier and Dom Malonga, and things began to look up. John McGinn, who had been quiet, began to exert an influence and Liam Henderson used the ball really well as Hibs began to turn the screw in the closing stages.

Good chances were created and missed and it looked like being one of those days. Then in the ninety-fourth minute, Queens cleared the ball deep into Hibs' half. Fraser Fyvie was closing in on possession when referee Brian Colvin stopped the game for an injury to a Queens player in his own penalty area. Colvin restarted the game with a drop ball which the player left to Liam Fontaine expecting him to kick it up the field to safety. Instead Fontaine brought the ball forward and a move developed that culminated in the impressive Anier playing in David Gray who delivered a superb cross ball.

Dominique Malonga met Gray's cross and headed the ball down and into the net. Easter Road erupted and Queen of the South erupted too as they felt that Hibs should not have kept possession after the referee had dropped the ball. None of the 9,000 odd Hibs fans inside the ground was the least bit concerned about that. They were just delighted that Hibs had snatched victory from the jaws of a draw and brought themselves level on points with Rangers.

After the game, I walked home with my son, daughter and grandson. As we got further away from the ground, we bumped into a couple of local worthies who both turned out to have Hibs sympathies. The first, an older man, asked us the score. When we told him, he replied with real feeling 'That's the best thing I've heard a' day.' The second was younger and was eating a fish supper out of the paper with great gusto. He clearly knew the result but recognising our colours, he shouted to us as he passed, 'Come oan the Hibs!'

There has been speculation that the 'rabbit' which Alan Stubbs is hoping to pull out of the hat in January might be either

Anthony Stokes or Scott Allan. Unfortunately, Ronny Deila the Celtic manager has made it clear that neither of these moves will take place, which is a great pity.

The fall-out from the Queen of the South match continues. Queens' Derek Lyle has been very vocal claiming that a Hibs player who wasn't on the bench or even stripped for action on Saturday challenged him to a fight in the tunnel at full time. Lyle hasn't named the Hibs man in question. The Queens' striker has claimed that he was more than ready to do battle as he is not a man to back down but says that Alan Stubbs intervened and advised him to be sensible and avoid trouble. He concurred with Stubbs' words of wisdom and eventually walked away.

Referee Brian Colvin has yet to submit a report on the goings on in the tunnel. It may be hard for him to do so as he probably didn't see what happened as he stayed on the pitch until the majority of players had left it. Hopefully everyone's thoughts will now turn back to football and the mammoth game with Rangers which will be played at Ibrox on the fourth last day of 2015.

Two former Hibs players were in the news today. Derek Riordan has posted a message on the career networking website Linkedin appealing for a club to give him a chance to reinvigorate his career. Derek is only thirty-two, has trained hard with Hibs for three months and is a very talented footballer. There must be some club out there that will give him a chance.

Darren Jackson, who was a tremendous player for Hibs in the 1990s, has been declared bankrupt with debts of £270,000 after a failed investment. Darren was very helpful to me when I was writing my book on Franck Sauzée. He had played against Sauzée and shared his thoughts on the great man with me. He also came along to the book launch and spoke really well when I interviewed him. I hope his financial affairs take a turn for the better soon.

It may be the season of goodwill but you wouldn't think so if you were reading the sports pages in the newspapers.

Derek Riordan has claimed that someone in football is sabotaging his career. He says that he is fit and raring to go and still has all his ability or as he himself rather prosaically put it, 'I haven't suddenly become crap.' Riordan reckons that someone is orchestrating a whispering campaign against him and wants a club to give him a chance. He was also speaking about current Scotland manager Gordon Strachan who was of course Derek's team boss at Celtic. Riordan made it clear that he was of the opinion that Strachan did not like him and that was a factor in his infrequent selection for first-team duty at Parkhead.

Alan Stubbs and Mark Warburton have also continued their war of words. Stubbs declared that if Warburton really didn't believe that Rangers had hit a bit of a form crisis then he was in denial. Warburton retorted that the only crisis which he had at present was trying to decide what to buy his wife for Christmas.

Meanwhile Hibs have signed a striker. He is twenty-nine-year-old Liverpudlian Chris Dagnall. Dagnall has signed until the end of the season. He has previously played for Tranmere, Rochdale, Barnsley and Leyton Orient. Most recently he has been playing in the Indian Premier League. He has scored over one hundred career goals but his scoring ratio of around one goal in every four games couldn't be described as prolific.

Hibs have lost 4–2 to Rangers at Ibrox. Jason Cummings gave Hibs the lead but two goals from Jason Holt and one from Nicky Clark put Rangers 3–1 up. Dominique Malonga got a goal back for Hibs but Martyn Waghorn's late goal gave Rangers a clear and deserved victory. Hibs were not at their best and gave the ball away too readily. Their defending was unconvincing too. Alan Stubbs had been winding up Rangers and their manager Mark Warburton in the lead up to the game but it was Warburton who had the last word. Hibs are now three points behind Rangers and three ahead of Falkirk at the half way point of the season.

I wasn't able to watch the game as I was visiting my brother-in-law Terry in hospital. Terry, a lifelong Hibee, has a particularly aggressive form of leukaemia and is not at all well. He is displaying unbelievable courage as he fights his illness. Normally a defeat to Rangers in a vital match would lead to me being seriously depressed. Today it didn't seem all that important in the greater scheme of things.

One positive from yesterday's game was the performance of Jason Cummings which, like his finish for Hibs' first goal, was right out of the top drawer. English clubs are now queuing up to sign him. Hibs must not sell him under any circumstances.

Falkirk have beaten Livingston and have gone above Hibs into second place albeit on goal difference and with one more game played.

My brother-in-law Terry's condition has worsened. We are all praying that this great Hibs supporter can win his fight for life but tragically it is looking increasingly unlikely that he will.

January 2016

League Cup Final Here We Come

Good start in Scottish Cup – one thousandth goal – the return of Stokes and Thomson – into League Cup final – busy January transfer window

It's the start of a new year but it's not a time of celebration for our family. Terry continues to fight for his life. On Tuesday afternoon, the doctors told Terry's immediate family that they expected him to survive for another twenty-four hours or, at the most, thirty-six. Terry's wife and children have maintained a vigil by his bedside ever since. Here we are seventy-two hours later and this incredibly brave man still refuses to release his grip on life. Terry's courage has been matched by his family's fortitude.

On the football front, Hibs are set to return to action. Raith Rovers will first-foot them at Easter Road. New signing Chris Dagnall will make his debut if the requisite paper work can be completed on time. One player who won't feature is Fraser

Fyvie, who has received a two-match ban for simulation in the incident in the Ibrox game that saw Rangers Andy Halliday sent off. Halliday aimed a kick at Fyvie and then barged into his chest. Fyvie's reaction was to clutch his head! He hasn't been at his best in recent games so the break may do him good. Against Rangers, Fyvie conceded possession for their first goal, feigned a head injury and got turned inside out by Martyn Waghorn for the final goal so, all in all, it wasn't his best day at the office. Fraser is a player who is full of running and industry and who never hides in games. Hibs are a better team when Fyvie is hard at work in the middle of the park and he will come again.

Alan Stubbs has scotched rumours that he was about to sign his former teammate Leon Osman from Everton. Osman is thirty-four now but would still represent a considerable coup in the transfer market. However, at his media conference, Stubbs poured cold water on the notion that Osman might come to Easter Road, pointing out that he had come on as a substitute for Everton as recently as their last match against Stoke City.

Terry lost his fight for life on the morning of Saturday 2 January. As a family, we are sadder than words can express. Terry supported Hibs all his life, having been taken to matches from an early age by his dad Arthur. He always bought his season ticket on the first day that seasons became available and bought shares both individually and through Hibernian Supporters' Limited during the club's recent share issue. Terry also had a programme collection going back over half a century which covered every Hibs home match in that time.

He sat with his older son Michael in the East Stand. His other son David is also a season ticket holder. Michael's son Francis and David's daughter Lois are Hibs Kids. When the Hibs Kids'

Parade took place at Easter Road earlier this season, I walked along the trackside with my daughter Lisa and grandson John. As we passed the part of the stand where Terry sat, we waved up to him. He gave us a cheery wave back. Now just a few short months later, he is no longer with us.

Hibs managed a win against Raith Rovers with Jason Cummings scoring the winner from the penalty spot. It was a laboured performance and not at all convincing. Rangers, on the other hand, went to Dumbarton and won 6–0. Falkirk won at Alloa. At full time, I looked over to where Terry used to sit, raised my arm and clenched my fist and said, 'That was for you Terry.'

I have taken a letter to Rod Petrie informing him of Terry's passing. When I got to Easter Road, the chairman wasn't available so I gave the letter to Frank Dougan in his role as supporter director and he was very sympathetic. Later today, I received a nice letter from Mr Petrie expressing his condolences, stating that the club will be represented at Terry's funeral and letting me know that there will be a tribute to Terry in the programme for the next home match against St Mirren. That letter was much appreciated.

When I was at Easter Road, first-team coach John Doolan brought Hibs' latest signing Niklas Gunnarsson into the reception area of the West Stand. Gunnarsson is apparently an attacking right-back who specialises in long throws. I was sitting with Frank Dougan when he came in and he walked over and shook hands with both of us, which was a nice touch.

Hibs are about to face Raith Rovers for the second time in seven days. This time the match will be a Scottish Cup tie at Stark's Park. Alan Stubbs has been talking about going two steps better than last season in pursuit of what he rightly calls 'The Holy

Grail'. That would be nice. It would be more than nice. It would be fantastic. Here's hoping. Normally, I would be intensely focused on tomorrow's events. In truth, I am still in mourning for Terry.

Today we gathered at Terry's house and shared memories of his life to help his older son Michael collect reflections to inform the eulogy to his dad, which he will deliver at Terry's requiem mass next week.

Many stories were shared, all of them happy. Then the Hibs score came through at 4.50pm. A 2–0 win, without Jason Cummings, but with Darren McGregor getting Hibs' 1000th Scottish Cup goal and Dominique Malonga getting the other, was more than acceptable. Maybe, just maybe, this will be Hibs' year. Surely if you score your 1000th goal in a competition, it must be your season to win it!

This morning, out for a walk, I met an old friend Peter Clark. Peter was in St Giles Supporters' branch in the sixties with his great friend and, friend of mine, Benny Small, when my wife Margaret and I travelled to games on the Eastern Branch bus. He said that he was heading for Kirkcaldy. He asked me if I was going to Stark's Park, but referring to our family get-together at Terry's, I told him that, for once on Scottish Cup day, my thoughts would be elsewhere.

Reflecting on a very satisfactory result at Stark's Park, I can't help thinking that there would be no more fitting epitaph for Terry than Hibs lifting the Scottish Cup in May.

Hibs' reward for victory at Stark's Park is an away tie at Tynecastle! Hearts are third in the Premiership and knocked out Aberdeen in the last round. A hostile reception, both on and off the field, no doubt lies in wait for the team in green and white when they travel to Gorgie in early February.

At least the club should receive welcome income from such a high-profile match-up. In the meantime some vital league games and a League Cup semi-final all have to be dealt with. It's a very difficult draw but if Hibs' name is on the cup, then they will come through.

Despite the earlier denials of the possibility of such a move by the Celtic manager Ronny Deila, there are again strong rumours linking Anthony Stokes with a return to Easter Road. That would be nice. He is an excellent footballer and a natural goal scorer. A double from Stokesy at Tynecastle in February would do very nicely indeed!

Terry's funeral has taken place. There was a large turnout at both St John's Church in Portobello and at Seafield Crematorium after the requiem mass. Terry's wife Pat and his children Michael, Louise and David made a splendid job of organising exactly the funeral Terry had said he wanted when we spoke to him in hospital as his illness became ever more serious. Michael spoke movingly about his dad in the church and Louise did the same at the crematorium. Father Jock Dalrymple, Terry's parish priest, conducted proceedings with dignity and compassion.

Rod Petrie, Leeann Dempster, Greig Mailer and Frank Dougan all represented Hibs at the funeral. They conducted themselves with care and respect and their attendance was much appreciated. When I spoke to Rod afterwards, he made reference to Terry 'belonging to the Hibernian family', a remark which really struck a chord with me.

It has been a quiet transfer window so far but things are beginning to warm up. Hibs have confirmed that they are allowing

Henri Anier to return to Dundee United. Anier did little to catch the eye in his few months at Easter Road. He spent a lot of time on the treatment table and his only significant contribution was the neat flick which he produced to set up Martin Boyle's equaliser against Falkirk.

Islam Feruz is expected to follow Anier through the exit door and go back to Chelsea. He arrived at Hibs with a big reputation but has totally failed to live up to it. He will be no loss.

Jordon Forster has gone to Plymouth Argyle on loan until the end of the season. His contract expires at that point but Hibs have already offered him a new deal. This is a clever move as it ensures that if Forster does move on in the summer, Hibs will be entitled to compensation. The excellent form of Liam Fontaine, Paul Hanlon and Darren McGregor have limited big Jordon's opportunities as have a succession of injuries. He said today that if he does move on at the end of the season, Hibs will always be in his heart, which is nice to hear.

I hope that all of the above activity is part of the process of clearing the decks for the arrival of Anthony Stokes. Kilmarnock, Inverness and Dundee United are also in for Stokes and there is interest too from south of the border. He has given no indication as yet as to what his destination might be. I very much hope that it is Easter Road.

Hibs have fought out their second 1–1 draw of the season with Falkirk, this time at the Westfield Stadium. It was a cagey and goalless first half in which Hibs dominated possession but lacked a cutting edge. Falkirk took the lead early in the second half with a classy goal from Blair Alston although Liam Fontaine won't be happy with the way he sold himself in the tackle just before Alston fired the ball home.

Hibs responded well and should have had a penalty when Luke Leahy dived in on John McGinn and made clear contact with him as McGinn drove into the penalty area. John Beaton the referee rejected Hibs' appeals but he shouldn't have done because it was a clear-cut spot kick. Ludicrously, Falkirk manager Peter Houston said after the game that McGinn had gone to ground too easily and was in danger of earning himself a reputation as a diver. McGinn, in fact, tried to stay on his feet despite Leahy clearly catching him. Alan Stubbs and every pundit including Liam Craig, Chris Sutton and Stephen Craigan said it was a definite penalty. All Houston succeeded in doing was making himself appear foolish.

Justice was done when Jason Cummings, with a typical poacher's finish, scored a seventy-third minute equaliser. Hibs had chances to win the match after that but failed to take them. Watching on from the stand were Anthony Stokes and Kevin Thomson, who are both expected to sign for Hibs next week. Stokes' arrival will be a major coup as he should be outstanding in the Championship. Thomson has been Dundee's captain this season and has left Dens Park by mutual consent because he feels his body can no longer stand up to the rigours of playing regularly in the top flight. He will combine coaching with playing in his third spell at Easter Road. I am sure that Alan Stubbs will use him sparingly but he remains what Alex Miller used to describe as a 'quality player'.

Peter Houston has apologised to John McGinn for suggesting that if he wasn't careful he would earn himself a reputation for going down too easily in the penalty area. Houston's apology followed on from his having watched television replays of the tackle on McGinn by Luke Leahy. He might have had the sense to view the footage first and then give his opinion. His unwarranted slur on such a fine and sporting young player as McGinn did him no credit at all.

There is still no confirmation of the signing of either Anthony Stokes or Kevin Thomson. Hopefully there have been no last-minute hitches and the deals will be done soon. Stokes hasn't played for Celtic for five months so he may find it difficult to hit the ground running. Thomson, if he signs, will add experience both on the pitch and in the dressing room.

Anthony Stokes has indeed become a Hibs player once more. His signing was confirmed today and it is excellent news. In the meantime, Derek Riordan, Stokes' former strike partner at Easter Road, has gone on trial to York City, managed by Jackie McNamara, at the bottom of English League 2. Riordan is much better than that but for some strange reason, although he is still only in his early thirties, he is finding it very hard to get a club. Unless his attitude is poor, which he denies, I find the whole thing very hard to understand.

Derek Riordan has been in the news again today. First, he said that he expects Anthony Stokes and Jason Cummings to score a 'barrow load of goals' together although he also stated that he didn't consider the duo to be the 'brightest'. Maybe Derek sees himself as a bit of an intellectual! The TSB Bank had gone to court in an attempt to repossess Riordan's home but the case has been put into abeyance as it appears that funds may be in place to pay the striker's mortgage arrears.

The aforementioned Stokes has also been in court. He was in Dublin to stand trial on the ludicrous-sounding charge of 'assaulting an Elvis impersonator'. The case was adjourned until

November due to the unavailability of one of the witnesses. Maybe Elvis had left the building!

I met Alex Cropley recently. Alex has just celebrated his sixty-fifth birthday, although it seems like no time at all since he was strutting his stuff in midfield for Hibs, Arsenal, Aston Villa and Scotland. He told me that Eric Stevenson is unwell. That is very sad news. Eric was a superb player – in the Davie Cooper mould but, in my opinion, better – and he is a lovely man. I really hope that he can overcome his illness and make a full recovery.

Anthony Stokes has given his first interview since returning to Easter Road and he spoke very well. He made it clear that, although he had quite a few clubs to choose from, signing for Hibs was always his preferred option. Describing Hibs as a 'great club', Stokes made it clear that he wants to play games and score goals and, by so doing, help Hibs to win the Championship. He is still hoping to win a place in Martin O'Neill's Ireland squad for the Euro 2016 Finals in France in the summer and he wants to convince Ronny Deila that he is good enough to figure in Celtic's first team next season. His pursuit of these twin targets can only be to Hibs' benefit. He didn't mention the Scottish Cup though and it would be nice to think that his goals could propel us towards that coveted trophy as well.

Kevin Thomson has signed for Hibs for the third time. The club's young players will profit from his coaching and the first team will be enhanced by his ability to retain possession. Hibs next face St Mirren at Easter Road. At the risk of repeating myself, this is a must-win game. Hibs drew with Saints the last time they met them at home and have to do better tomorrow. I would definitely play Anthony Stokes from the start.

He is certainly short of match practice but class, as they say, is permanent.

There is talk that Dominique Malonga is on his way to Italy. I like Dom. He is a player of quality but he isn't inclined to over-exert himself and his tally for the season to date of six goals in a team enjoying as much possession and creating as many chances as Hibs, should be better.

Hibs have beaten St Mirren 3–1. The team's performance was very similar to how they have played in most other home games over the last season and a half. They monopolised possession, dominated territorially, created lots of chances and missed most of them or were denied by heroic goalkeeping and defending and conceded an avoidable goal.

Liam Henderson who played very well displaying great awareness and unveiling a repertoire of flicks and neat touches put Hibs in front with an early free kick which he curled beautifully into the top corner of Jamie Langfield's net and John McGinn put the finishing touch to a lovely move just before half time to give Hibs a clear lead. However, Hibs being Hibs, they gave away a needless free kick on the edge of the box in first-half stoppage time. Mark Oxley got his positioning all wrong and his attempt to save Stevie Mallon's less than rocket-powered shot was not impressive.

So, once again, the second half was tense with opportunities squandered, great saves by Langfield and goal line clearances. Anthony Stokes, on for his second Hibs' debut as a substitute, finally allowed the fans to breathe easily when he netted from close range after excellent work by James Keatings to put the game beyond doubt in the eighty-eighth minute.

Stokes looked a class apart when he came on with twenty minutes remaining. He found space, employed a secure first touch, used the ball skilfully and was in the right place to claim a typical striker's goal. Dylan McGeouch, who is such a good and important player, was missing once more. One can only assume he was injured yet again.

There was a very nice tribute to my brother-in-law Terry in the match programme. It was very poignant to sit at Easter Road where Terry was a fixture for every home game for over half a century and look at his photo in the programme while realising that he will never again be able to shout on his beloved Hibees. The club has done a great job in honouring Terry's memory.

Hibs today made their fifth signing of the transfer window. They have certainly invested heavily over the past few weeks and deserve great credit for doing so. To be honest, I am not sure where the funds are coming from.

The latest signing is twenty-one-year-old, six foot five Finnish goalkeeper Otso Virtanen. Virtanen has signed a three-and-a-half-year deal so the club obviously thinks highly of him. I watched him being interviewed on Hibs TV and he seems quite a character. He gave very direct, concise answers to every question he was asked and avoided all the usual clichés that footballers come out with when being interviewed on arrival at a new club. When asked if he was finding the weather in Scotland similar to that in his home country on the mildest day of the winter with temperatures of 15 °C, he replied that this was like a summer's day in Finland. He added that when he had left for Edinburgh, the Finnish thermometers had been reading -25 °C! If Virtanen is as adept at keeping goal as he is at expressing himself verbally then Mark Oxley will eventually have a much needed rival for the number one slot.

There was an interesting interview with Liam Craig in the Sunday papers. Craig will, of course, line up against Hibs for St

Johnstone in next weekend's League Cup semi-final at Tynecastle. He said that he expected a warm reception from some Hibs supporters in the semi but hoped that the majority would respect the efforts that he always put in on the club's behalf. He clearly retains a lot of affection for Hibs and has remained friendly with David Gray and Liam Fontaine. I will certainly have nothing but goodwill for Liam on Saturday (as long as he doesn't play too well) because he gave his all for our club. Unfortunately, that all wasn't good enough. When he played against Hibs for St Johnstone prior to joining up at Easter Road, he invariably performed well and scored quite a few goals. He never managed to reproduce that level of performance in a green and white jersey.

Maurice Malpas was another who was reflecting on his time with Hibs in the weekend press. It was very obvious from what Malpas said that he and Terry Butcher had totally lost the dressing room by the end of their spells at Easter Road.

They clearly hadn't considered the possibility that Hibs might go down and, when that possibility edged towards reality, things were too far gone to stem the tide. Malpas and Butcher ended up relying on players whom they had earmarked to be cleared out at the end of the season – and to whom they had communicated that fact – to bail them out of trouble. That was clearly not football management of the highest order.

Dominique Malonga has reached an agreement with Hibs for his contract to be terminated. There is interest in Dom from Italy and England and I am sure that it won't be long before he finds a new club. He is a talented player who has scored some fine goals for Hibs, most notably his outstanding solo effort against Aberdeen in the League Cup. There is no doubt, though, that he is a luxury player. Some games he looks in the mood but in other matches his interest level seems considerably lower. With a scrap for promotion and a battle for cup glory on the horizon, Alan Stubbs needs strikers who will give absolutely everything in every game. He clearly feels that he has this with Jason Cummings, Anthony Stokes, Chris Dagnall, James Keatings and Martin Boyle. There is also Jamie Insall in reserve. Insall is currently on loan at East Fife.

The situation with Farid El Alagui is less clear. Farid hasn't started a first-team game this season and also missed most of last season through injury. If he had been able to stay fit, Farid would have been a great signing. Unfortunately, as was the case with his last club, Brentford, Farid has proved to be susceptible to injury. I fear that his days at Easter Road are numbered.

Kevin Thomson met the media today and cut an impressive figure. He spoke more like a manager than a player! Kevin wants to help Hibs win promotion as this would exorcise the ghost of the disastrous relegation which he shared in in May 2014 and he is also keen to lift a cup with Hibs as he has played in two losing finals during his previous spells at the club and missed out in the 5–1 League Cup Final triumph over Kilmarnock in 2007, as he had been transferred to Rangers shortly before this game took place. Let's hope that he can achieve both of his twin ambitions.

Dominique Malonga has signed for an Italian Serie B club and Hibs have received an 'undisclosed fee', which I am sure will not amount to very much. Dom's message to Hibs fans was 'Au revoir. Merci Hibs'. Thank you too, Dominique. You were popular at Easter Road and all Hibs fans wish you well.

Tommy Wright, the St Johnstone manager, is really working hard at the mind games before the upcoming League Cup semi-final. The SPFL allocated Hibs an additional 600 tickets for the match having originally promised them to St Johnstone. Their reason for this change of mind is that if St Johnstone fans are given the tickets, they will have to sit close to the Hibs support and this will raise safety and segregation issues. They should really have thought of that before making promises to Saints. However, Wright is playing the situation up for all that it's worth saying that his club are used to being 'trampled on' by the bigger clubs and the authorities, and that they will use this latest example of that as motivation. I am sure they will. Hopefully Hibs, with three out of four stands at Tynecastle filled with green and white, won't lack motivation either.

Tommy Wright is also trying to portray his team as underdogs. I am not sure what logic he is applying here as Saints have won the Scottish Cup and have finished in the top six of the Premiership regularly in recent years while Hibs are spending their second season in the Championship.

Talking of League Cup semi-finals against St Johnstone, Abdessalam Benjelloun, aka Benji, has just celebrated his thirty-first birthday. Benji scored an insouciant goal against Saints at Tynecastle to clinch Hibs' win there in 2007 and went on to score two superb goals in the 5–1 victory over Kilmarnock in the final. He was an enigmatic talent who had lots of ability but didn't make the most of it on a consistent basis. My favourite Benji moment was when he scored the winning goal in a derby against Hearts at Easter Road and ran the full length of the field to celebrate in front of the Hearts end. After the game, when it looked like he might find himself in a bit of disciplinary hot water for doing this, he claimed that it was common practice in his home country of Morocco!

It has been quite a winter with non-stop rain and seven storms battering the country since November. Yesterday the latest storm in line, Storm Gertrude, wrought havoc across the country. There was a gust of wind recorded at 105 mph! League Cup semi-final day has dawned calm with snow on the ground. The match is not in doubt though.

What is doubtful is who will win this hugely talked-up encounter between Hibs and St Johnstone. Tommy Wright has done most of the talking. Alan Stubbs, in contrast to his previous contretemps with Mark Warburton, has been fairly restrained.

Derek Riordan has signed a contract with York City. In his usual outspoken manner, he has said that he expects to deliver goals and also act as a playmaker. No pressure there, then. I still wish that Derek was following in the footsteps of Kevin Thomson and beginning a third stint at Easter Road. We won't be able to count on Derek's goals today but we do have Anthony Stokes, Jason Cummings, James Keatings and Chris Dagnall which is, by anyone's standards, an estimable strike force.

Hibs have qualified for the League Cup Final and deservedly so. St Johnstone were beaten 2–1 at Tynecastle in a game which Hibs dominated throughout. They played really well with the midfield quartet of Dylan McGeouch, Fraser Fyvie, Liam Henderson and the brilliant John McGinn all highly impressive.

Hibs scored first when Liam Henderson went down in the penalty area and, to the fury of the Saints defenders who clearly believed that Hendo had gone down too easily, referee Steven McLean pointed to the spot. Television replays later suggested that the Perth players may have had a case. Jason Cummings duly slotted the penalty home, sending goalkeeper Alan Mannus the wrong way in the process. St Johnstone equalised within three minutes from a Joe Shaughnessy header. Hibs created several excellent chances in the second half but only converted one when McGinn fired home a twenty-yard daisy cutter with quarter of an hour to go.

Saints did exert some late pressure but neither David Wotherspoon nor Liam Craig could score against their old team and, in the end, Hibs held out fairly comfortably. This was one big occasion when Hibs definitely turned up and they proved conclusively and not for the first time that they are more than capable of holding their own in the Premiership.

Hibs opponents in the final on Sunday 13 March will be Ross County who beat Celtic 3–1 in the other semi-final at Hampden. Celtic had a player sent off early in the first half and Leigh Griffiths missed a penalty late in the game so it was very much County's day. The team from Dingwall should not be underestimated but Hibs will feel that they have a real chance of lifting silverware for the first time in nine years. A final against Celtic would have been a very big ask. A match against a greatly improved Ross County will be far from easy but is definitely more winnable. If Ronny Deila isn't sacked as Celtic manager after today he will be a very lucky man. His support and his budget are significantly bigger than that of any other SPFL Premiership club yet he has once again come up short.

Being at Tynecastle was an interesting experience. We sat in the main stand which is around one hundred years old. It felt like it. It was claustrophobic with a roof which hung so low that it blotted out the sky and all of the other stands in the ground apart from their bottom few rows. The toilet facilities could only be described as basic. Easter Road is a superb, modern football stadium and yesterday's experience made you very much appreciate that. Some Hibs fans sang, to the tune of the Beach Boys' 'Sloop John B', 'Tynecastle's a sh***hole, I want to go home.' Well they'll have to go back there next Sunday for a crucial

Scottish Cup Tie and, before that, Hibs travel to Cappielow for the latest in the team's series of must-win league matches.

Rangers have beaten Falkirk 1–0 at Ibrox, courtesy of a ninety-first-minute goal from Billy King whom they had signed on loan from Hearts only a day earlier. They are now eight points ahead of Hibs with an extra game played and it is imperative that that deficit is reduced to five points.

February 2016

A Championship Stumble

Fightback in Gorgie – Stubbs linked with Celtic – famous cup win over Hearts – slip up in the Championship

The January transfer window ended quietly for Hibs. There was speculation that they might make a move for Stefan Scougall of Sheffield United but nothing came of it. The earlier captures of Anthony Stokes, Chris Dagnall, Kevin Thomson, Otso Virtanen and Niklas Gunnarsson represent an impressive haul and really no transfer activity was necessary on deadline day. When asked prior to the window closing if there would be any 'comings or goings' at Easter Road, Alan Stubbs answered with a smile, 'No, Cummings won't be going.' Jason stays for the foreseeable future and that has to be good news for all Hibs fans.

Hearts had a busy and productive transfer deadline day. They signed Don Cowie from Wigan, Abiola Dauda, a Nigerian striker with a decent record, and John Souttar from Dundee

United. They let Morgaro Gomis go on loan to Motherwell and, amazingly, sold Osman Sow, who was out of contract in the summer, to a Chinese club for a seven-figure fee.

Apparently Sow can still play in Sunday's Scottish Cup derby as the Chinese transfer window doesn't close until 26 February. Typical Hearts luck in being able to have their cake and eat it. If that isn't bad enough, it has been confirmed that Sunday's match will be refereed by Craig Thomson. This is the man who contributed significantly to the margin of Hearts' 5–1 Scottish Cup final win in 2012. Let's hope history doesn't repeat itself in terms of the result on Sunday.

Rangers have signed the talented Michael O'Halloran from St Johnstone and he will be in their squad when they travel to face Raith. Hibs, of course also play in midweek when they go to Cappielow. A Rangers win and a Hibs defeat would see the light blues' lead at the top of the table increase to eleven points which is unthinkable.

Alan Stubbs has done a magnificent job since coming to Hibs but, as he says himself, he has achieved nothing yet. His most important target is promotion back to the Premiership (although either or both of the cups would be wonderful) and games like the Morton match will go a long way towards deciding whether Hibs can return to their rightful place in Scottish football or whether they will be consigned to second-tier obscurity for a third consecutive season. I know that I say this before every league match – and I only say it because it is true – but victory for Hibs in Greenock is absolutely essential. Hopefully, the wild winds with which Storm Henry, the second major storm to hit the country in seventy-two hours, has battered Scotland will have died down by kick-off time. Morton gave Rangers a tough game last week and they will push Hibs all the way. Hibs have to be on their mettle right from the word go. It's going to be tense.

It was extremely tense but Hibs came through. They ground out a 1–0 win and got those oh-so-vital three points. Alan Stubbs felt that the team should have made things more comfortable for themselves but, as so often before, there was a failure to convert possession into goals. Rangers also won 1–0 at Raith. Rovers manager Ray McKinnon was furious that the referee had chalked off what he considered to be a perfectly good goal. Fraser Fyvie (knee) and Liam Fontaine (hamstring) picked up injuries at Cappielow. Hopefully, they will be fit for the Scottish Cup derby.

Fraser Fyvie will be out for at least four weeks. His industry will be missed against Hearts. There is still a possibility that Liam Fontaine might make the game. Anthony Stokes says that he expects a hostile reaction at Tynecastle. He claimed that that is the reaction he normally gets when he plays there but he added that the personal abuse he gets from the Hearts fans doesn't bother him as he has usually scored in his matches in Gorgie and ended up on the winning side. Let's hope both of those things happen again at the weekend.

What an afternoon at Tynecastle. Hibs left Liam Fontaine on the bench as a precaution while Hearts decided not to risk Osman Sow in case he received an injury and jeopardised his big-money move to China. Sow was presented to the crowd before the game, as was Paolo Sergio, Hearts manager when they won the 5–1 Scottish Cup Final. These were moves clearly aimed at building the pre-match hostility to Hibs even more and unsettling them before the game even kicked off.

When the match did start, Hibs played well and had the better of the opening exchanges. Dylan McGeouch went off with yet another groin injury and David Gray also had to leave the field. Kevin Thomson and Niklas Gunnarsson replaced them and both went on to play very well. Hearts also had to make two substitutions losing Prince Buaben and Alim Ozturk to injury.

Just when it looked like Hibs were comfortable, disaster struck, as it has so often before in Gorgie. Calum Paterson misdirected a cross into Hibs' box. The obvious thing for Lewis Stevenson to do was to control the ball and play it out of defence. For some unaccountable reason, he stooped almost to ground level and headed the ball straight to Arnaud Djoum who despatched an unstoppable twenty-yard shot past Mark Oxley. Worse was to follow. Another Paterson cross came into the middle. It was much more accurate this time and Hibs marking was slack. Sam Nicholson collected the ball in space and shot low past Oxley.

Two-nil down at half time, it was looking ominous for Hibs but to their great credit, they kept fighting. Hearts didn't help themselves by being content to hold what they had while trying to add to their lead on the break. Hibs looked like exiting from the cup despite their best efforts, when in the eightieth minute, Jason Cummings looped a brilliant header over Neil Alexander. It was a very similar goal to one scored against Henry Smith at Easter Road by Steve Archibald in the late 1980s. Hibs kept on coming and, in the ninety-first minute, Darren McGregor fired in a great header from a John McGinn corner but Alexander made a brilliant reflex save. Paul Hanlon reacted quickest to the loose ball and steered it into the net with his right foot to unleash scenes of euphoria in the Hibs end behind the goal.

The drama didn't end there. In the ninety-fourth and final minute, Hearts won a corner. Their central defender Błażej Augustyn won the header and bulleted the ball for goal. While Mark Oxley remained motionless, Kevin Thomson headed the ball off the line. In the ensuing melee, Hibs blocked two more goal-bound efforts before getting the ball clear. Thomson said after the game that if Hibs had conceded a late goal after clawing back to parity, it would have been 'typical Hibs'. He was right, but thankfully the team held on for another richly deserved draw that felt like a win.

Another member of the Thomson clan, referee Craig, had a surprisingly good game. For once, Hibs fans had no grounds for complaint where this particular official was concerned.

Darren McGregor who played really well gave a superb interview after the game. He described Kevin Thomson as playing like a 'young whippersnapper' and said that Jason Cummings' ability to score such a fine header was down to the fact that his hair was rock hard as he 'puts a bottle of spray on it every day'.

It was a great fighting performance from Hibs and to leave Tynecastle still in the cup especially after having been two goals down so late in the game was a great feeling. It's when something like that happens that you start to think that this just might be Hibs' year to win the Scottish. Mind you, we have had these feelings before and we all know where they have taken us.

Hibs will play Inverness Caledonian Thistle at Easter Road in the quarter-final of the Scottish Cup if they can defeat Hearts in the replay. The replay will not be televised live as it clashes with Champions League matches. Television companies are not allowed to show other games in direct competition with Champions League encounters. This will be the first Edinburgh derby not to be shown live on television for ten years. The loss of a TV match fee will cost each club £85,000. Hopefully, this will be offset by a full house in the stadium.

Worryingly, the *Daily Record* is linking Celtic – who are struggling under Ronny Deila (they only beat East Kilbride 2–0 yesterday)

– with a move for Alan Stubbs. Their story was headlined, 'Time for Celts to move from sub-standard to Stubbs standard'. Stubbs is doing a fantastic job and, if he left, it would be a huge blow to Hibs.

The last Hibs manager to be spirited away to Parkhead was the great Jock Stein back in 1965. We most certainly do not want to see history repeating itself. Hibs were on course to achieve a league and Scottish Cup double when the Big Man left and they ended up winning neither.

Tickets for the Scottish Cup replay against Hearts have only just gone on sale at Easter Road. Already Hibs have sold 10,000 tickets for the match which is amazing. Charlie Reid of the Proclaimers has appeared on Sky Sports to say that he believed that the money coming in through the sale of shares at Hibs has been instrumental in allowing Alan Stubbs to strengthen his team, which I am sure is true.

Lewis Stevenson will make his 298th first-team appearance for Hibs at Livingston in the Championship at the weekend. He will then play his 299th match against Hearts in the Scottish Cup replay. His 300th game should have been against Alloa at home but he will miss it through suspension which means that his landmark moment will come in the home game against Morton that follows the Alloa match. Lewis did not have his best game at Tynecastle on Sunday but he has been having another excellent season and has been a magnificent servant to Hibs – the epitome of both consistency and application.

The Scottish Cup replay against Hearts is sold out, which is great. For the moment, though, the focus is on the next league game against Livingston at the Tony Macaroni Arena.

David Gray and Dylan McGeouch are close to returning to action. Gray is managing an ongoing niggling knee injury while McGeouch has suffered the latest in a long line of muscle strains. This one is described, following a scan, as 'slight'.

Livingston are just above the relegation zone and are in a false position. Only Hibs' best, with what looks like being a weakened team, will be good enough. To repeat the mantra of this cut-throat Championship season, Stubbs' men simply cannot afford any slip-ups. Rangers' relentless consistency means that if Hibs want to keep pace with them then they have to keep winning. It's as simple as that.

Rangers drew at Alloa and Falkirk shared the points at home to Raith before Hibs took the field at Livingston for their 5.15pm kick off. Presented with a great chance to gain points on Rangers and move further away from Falkirk, they failed to do either and had to settle for a less than acceptable 0–0 draw. The weather was dreadful with snow swirling around throughout the game and Livingston were organised and spirited but Hibs didn't do nearly enough.

While Hibs had to cope with a punishing encounter, Hearts put their feet up. Their match at Tynecastle with Partick Thistle was called off because the pitch was waterlogged. No other senior game in Britain was postponed so the Jambos' luck continues to hold. They will definitely go into next week's Scottish Cup replay as the fresher team.

Rangers and Falkirk both dropping two points on Saturday was a very rare occurrence and presented Hibs with a great opportunity to gain vital ground. Sadly, they blew their chance. Hibs have been grinding out results in recent weeks but have only really been at their best on one occasion and that was in the League Cup semi-final against St Johnstone. At the Tony

Macaroni Arena, we got neither a quality performance nor the desired result.

Hibs just have to raise their game when Hearts come to Easter Road. Fraser Fyvie is still out and Dylan McGeouch is, according to his manager, 'touch and go'. McGeouch is a superb footballer and Hibs really miss him when he is unfit, which he quite often is. He seems susceptible to muscle strains in the groin area and seems to be one of these players who is only prepared to take the field when he considers himself 100% fit. It would be a bonus if he plays against Hearts but I don't think he will.

The weather forecast is for heavy rain and wind. These conditions will suit Hearts' physical approach and I know that they will press Hibs when they are in possession much more than they did in the second half at Tynecastle when they allowed them back into the game by lying back and soaking up pressure. Three days after the first cup match with Hibs, Hearts went up to Dingwall and beat Ross County 3–0. They are a strong, resilient team and will once again set Hibs a major challenge.

Hibs have beaten Hearts 1–0 to advance to the quarter-final of the Scottish Cup. It was quite a match. Jason Cummings, scoring against Hearts for the fourth game in a row, gave Hibs an early lead. A neat passing movement ended with Marvin Bartley sliding in David Gray whose pinpoint cross was met with a side-foot volley from Cummings.

Neil Alexander in the Hearts goal was left totally helpless by this accomplished finish. Jason ran behind the goal where the Hearts fans were congregated to celebrate. This was the obvious thing to do as that was the end he had scored at. He didn't leave the pitch but stood with hands raised in triumph in a totally non-inflammatory manner. Nonetheless, John Beaton, the referee, chose to caution him.

Hibs dominated the rest of the half with John McGinn and Anthony Stokes causing Hearts all sorts of problems. They couldn't increase their lead, though, and Hearts in a rare foray up field had the ball in the net. The linesman flagged it offside.

In the second half, Hibs made the same error that Hearts had committed at Tynecastle in the first tie. They lay back and soaked up the pressure. This mainly consisted of a succession of high balls pumped into the box. Hearts did get the ball in the net again but once more an offside decision in Hibs' favour was given. Hibs still managed to create more clear-cut chances. Liam Henderson didn't make the most of a shooting opportunity created skilfully by McGinn, Cummings shot straight at Alexander after being set up by Stokes and substitute Danny Carmichael shot past when he might have scored after another excellent set up by Stokes.

Then Hearts centre-half Błażej Augustyn was sent off for a second yellow card when he threw the ball down in protest at a decision by the referee. Jason Cummings followed him down the tunnel two minutes later. He overran the ball to concede a goal kick to Hearts. He then flicked the ball back into play well away from the Hearts goalkeeper. Hearts pointedly left the ball lying where it came to a rest near the right touchline and crowded round referee Beaton who evened things up by producing a second yellow and then a red card for Cummings. It was a silly thing for Jason to do but a very soft booking and subsequent sending off.

Mr Beaton then decided that there should be five minutes of added on time. In the last of those minutes, Martin Boyle – on for Liam Henderson – made a seventy-yard lung-bursting run. He laid the ball on a plate for James Keatings who had just replaced Stokes but unaccountably Keats managed to shank the ball horribly wide of an empty net. Seconds later, referee Beaton blew for full time and Easter Road erupted into mass celebrations.

Alan Stubbs has now gone five derby games unbeaten against Hearts which is the best record of any Hibs manager since Alex McLeish. He would have been pleased with his team last night. John McGinn again combined creativity and energy and it is no surprise that he is being tipped for a call up by Scotland. Darren McGregor was immense at centre-half and big Marvin Bartley bossed the middle of the park. Anthony Stokes must have impressed the Republic of Ireland assistant manager Roy Keane who was watching from the stand. His leading of the line was exemplary and he could not have worked any harder.

After the match, Cliff Pyke on Hibs TV said to Alan Stubbs, 'I don't know about you Alan but after that I will have to go and lie down in a darkened room.' Stubbs replied that he hadn't felt nervous at any point! He must have been the only one of a Hibs persuasion who didn't. Around us the tension was palpable and both Kevin Thomson and Darren McGregor described the last ten minutes as the most nerve-wracking of their long careers.

Thomson spoke after the game about when he was released by Terry Butcher after Hibs' relegation. He revealed that Gary Locke had offered him the chance to sign for Hearts. He was out of work so he considered the offer. Having considered it, he then signed for Dundee! McGregor described the win over Hearts as the best of his career. Hopefully, Darren, there will be even better days and nights to come. Put Saturday 21 May in your diary right now.

This was Hibs' first Scottish Cup replay win over Hearts since 1877 so it was a historic victory indeed. Robbie Neilson said after the game that Hearts had lost the tie in the last ten minutes of the first game at Tynecastle. He was absolutely right. Amazingly, Hearts fans are calling for Neilson to be sacked after last night. Since taking over, he has brought them from the Championship to the Premiership at the first time of asking despite having to compete with Hibs and Rangers and currently has them sitting third in the top league. I am not sure what more they can possibly expect.

For a Hibs fan, there is nothing better than beating Hearts. To do it in a Scottish Cup tie after a famous comeback in the original match is even better. Seeing the Hibees lifting the Scottish Cup at Hampden in May might just surpass it, though.

Hibs have this season defeated Dundee United, Aberdeen, St Johnstone and Hearts of the Premiership in cup competitions. This proves that we belong in the top echelon of Scottish football. Getting back there will not be easy. Starting with Alloa and then following on with Morton, Queen of the South and Dumbarton, Hibs face four testing league games in the next two weeks before they play Inverness in the Scottish Cup quarterfinal. Alan Stubbs will have to make full use of his squad and hope that Fraser Fyvie and Dylan McGeouch, who didn't feature last night, regain fitness sooner rather than later.

Having now watched the television highlights of the derby, I have a couple of thoughts to share. The first is to confirm that the officials got both calls correct when they disallowed Hearts' offside goals. John Beaton was also right to send off Jason Cummings. He had no need to kick the ball away and put himself in danger. Błażej Augustyn, on the other hand, was probably unlucky to go as he looked to be throwing the ball back to the spot where a free kick had been awarded.

Secondly, the singing of 'Sunshine on Leith' at full time was memorably spine-tingling. It was fantastic to be part of at the match and great to watch again afterwards. Let's hope that we hear our anthem a few more times before the end of the season as that will mean that we've won some notable victories and maybe a trophy or two.

At 106, Sam Martinez is Hibs' oldest living supporter. He saw his first Hibs match seventy-four years ago! By my calculations, he missed the 8–1 victory over Rangers in 1941 by one year. He reckons this could be Hibs' year to lift the Scottish Cup. Mind you, he says that every year. Like Sam, though, I am starting to feel optimistic!

Hibs have three players suspended for the Scottish Cup quarter final against Inverness Caledonian Thistle. Marvin Bartley, Jason Cummings and Paul Hanlon are all out and they will all be missed. By scoring in four successive derbies, Jason has joined some excellent company, as the last two players to achieve this feat are Alex Cropley and Lawrie Reilly.

Rangers' top scorer Martyn Waghorn has injured his knee and is out for a few weeks. That is not good news for the player but very good news for Hibs. Anthony Stokes has once again courted media controversy by posting a selfie on Instagram of himself and a well-known character who has had his share of trouble with the law. Stokes is a hugely talented footballer and I just wish he would concentrate on his football and on delivering on the pitch week in, week out. I really believe that keeping away from the media spotlight when he's away from work would help him be the best he can be on the field of play.

The Hibs vs. Alloa game at Easter Road is live on Sky Sports. I think Alan Stubbs will ring the changes to freshen the team up and to give some players a much needed and well deserved break. While it makes sense to shuffle his pack, Stubbs will need to make sure that the eleven players who take the field are capable of beating what will be an organised and committed Alloa side. The Wasps held Rangers to a draw recently and were only a few minutes away from beating them so Hibs can't underestimate them. After last week's slip up at Livingston, nothing less than three points will do. So close is the battle for promotion between Rangers, Hibs and Falkirk that every league match is crucial.

Hibs have comfortably beaten Alloa 3–0 at Easter Road. That was good news. What was even more impressive though was the fact that Alan Stubbs had made seven changes to the team which had beaten Hearts earlier in the week. In came Niklas Gunnarsson, Liam Fontaine, Dylan McGeouch, Martin Boyle, Danny Carmichael, Chris Dagnall and James Keatings. Rests were given to David Gray, Darren McGregor, Kevin Thomson, John McGinn, Jason Cummings and Anthony Stokes. Lewis Stevenson was suspended.

Boyle scored twice and Carmichael scored the other. Both played very well as did Marvin Bartley once more and the outstanding McGeouch and Henderson. Hibs could have scored a few more but careless finishing and over-elaboration contributed to a number of missed opportunities. This was though definitely one of the less nerve-wracking home matches. Unfortunately, both Falkirk and Rangers have won again too so nothing has changed at the top of the Championship. Next up for Hibs is Morton.

Lewis Stevenson will make his 300th appearance for Hibs when he takes the field against Morton at Easter Road. Lewis' commitment and consistency have been highly impressive. He deserves to mark his special occasion with a victory and I very much hope that he does.

Alan Stubbs says that he is hopeful that Jason Cummings will sign a new contract for Hibs. An improved deal is on the table and Stubbs believes that it will be in Jason's best interests for him to sign it. He did add, though, that the player's agent may feel differently.

Hibs' quarter-final Scottish Cup tie against Inverness Caley Thistle will be played on Sunday 6 March. The game is live on BBC television. I hope this doesn't stop a bumper crowd turning out for what should be a cracking match.

Alan Stubbs says that despite the relentless schedule his players are facing and the pressure on them to win every match, the mood among the squad is 'relaxed'. With another crucial encounter in prospect, I hope that they are not too relaxed.

What a disaster! Morton have beaten Hibs (who were pretty much at full strength) 3–0. Hibs started well and missed a few chances (Jason Cummings was the main culprit). They also had a goal chalked off. Morton then took the lead with a header from a corner into Hibs' six-yard box while Mark Oxley and his defenders competed with each other to see who could be the most leaden-footed and least aware. Morton scored again just after half time when Oxley spilled a cross and went three ahead in sixty-three minutes after Darren McGregor had been caught in possession.

Morton were hugely committed, passed the ball well, defended as though their lives depended on it and broke at pace. Hibs were sluggish, slow, again over-elaborate in their build up and very poor at the back. I just don't think that Mark Oxley is good enough. I hope Otso Virtanen plays at Dumbarton at the weekend. In his online *Evening News* match report last night, David Hardie described Hibs' performance as 'abject' and said that Morton 'ran them ragged'. He was right on both counts.

It looks very much like the play-offs for Hibs now as I can't see Rangers throwing away the eight-point lead which they currently hold. It's very disappointing indeed. It's a real shame that such a wholehearted and loyal player as the estimable Lewis Stevenson couldn't mark his 300th appearance for Hibs with a victory.

The feeling of shock from the comprehensive and unexpected defeat to Morton hasn't worn off and yet once more as Alan Stubbs puts it, 'It's time to go again.' Hibs travel to Dumbarton to meet opponents with a point to prove. Dumbarton were well and truly turned over by Dundee in the Scottish Cup during the week and will be determined to get back on track. They will remember that they beat Hibs at home in the first game of the season and will do what Morton did on Wednesday and what every team which comes up against Hibs in the Championship does, they will play out of their skin, press non-stop, defend desperately and look to score on the break. Unless Rangers implode, which is unlikely to happen, Hibs are playing for second place now and Falkirk are breathing down their necks.

It will be interesting to see what team Alan Stubbs puts out today. Both Dylan McGeouch and Danny Carmichael are experiencing groin problems again, Liam Henderson needs a rest and Mark Oxley could be dropped. Hibs have signed seventeen-year-old left-back Sean Mackie from Raith Rovers for £25,000 on a four-and-a-half-year deal. Hearts were keen on Mackie too but he chose to go to Easter Road.

Hibs have launched another share issue for supporters. The video promoting the launch is very well done and features an excellent voice-over from Leeann Dempster. It is just a pity that the share issue was unveiled the day after Hibs' first defeat of 2016 which wasn't ideal timing.

Hibs have had another bitterly disappointing result. They have gone down 3–2 to Dumbarton, losing to the Sons for the second time this season. Hibs' performance pretty much summed up the reasons why they will not now win automatic promotion. The defence was poor again and in attack Hibs missed a host of opportunities. They had sixteen corners to Dumbarton's one!

Salt was rubbed into Hibs' wounds by two of the goals against them being scored by ex-Jambos Christian Nade and Darren Barr. Disgracefully, Nade made the 5–1 gesture to the crowd as he left the field.

After the game, Alan Stubbs said, 'We contributed significantly to our own downfall ... We had enough chances to win two games.' There was no place in the team or on the bench today for Anthony Stokes, Dylan McGeouch or David Gray. Paul Hanlon left the field with a swollen knee, which sounds ominous. Falkirk and Rangers have won again so Hibs are eleven points behind the Gers and only two points ahead of the Bairns. It is all very worrying and depressing.

Hibs haven't played really well for a few weeks now but have managed to grind out results. Since Christmas, though, the performances haven't matched the results with the exception of the two cup matches with Hearts and the League Cup semi-final against St Johnstone. In the last two games, neither performances nor points have been forthcoming. The team has had a gruelling schedule which is probably starting to tell but no one expected the defeats to Morton and Dumbarton.

March 2015

The Stumble Becomes a Fall

More losses in the league – Inverness draw – League Cup final disappointment – victory in the Highlands – defeat in Kirkcaldy

Hibs' dismal run has been extended. They have now lost in Dumfries as their unrelenting two-games-per-week schedule continues. Hibs totally dominated the match against Queen of the South but managed to lose 1–0. Ironically Queens' goal came from Andy Murdoch, a Rangers player on loan, whose goal was his first since moving to Palmerston Park. Rangers keep on winning and are away out of sight of Hibs now, a full fourteen points over the horizon. Falkirk drew with St Mirren and, by doing so, closed the gap on Hibs to a single point. The race for second place is well and truly on.

Alan Stubbs professed himself 'baffled' as to how Hibs have lost three league matches in a row after previously suffering only one defeat in twenty-eight games. He should be able to work it out. When Jason Cummings is scoring regularly, Hibs usually win, albeit more narrowly than should be the case. When Cummings goes off the boil, which he has in the last few matches, Hibs struggle to score. The defence is far from impregnable and the goalkeeper can be suspect so Hibs are always liable to lose matches when Jason doesn't deliver the goods.

Cummings is suspended for Sunday's Scottish Cup tie against Inverness. The other forward options are Anthony Stokes, who scored in his first two games back at Hibs but hasn't looked like doing so since, James Keatings, who hasn't scored since November, and Chris Dagnall, who hasn't scored at all since signing. Add to that the fact that Marvin Bartley is also suspended and Paul Hanlon is out for a month with a thigh injury and prospects for the weekend look much less promising than they did after the great victory over Hearts such a short time ago. One consoling thought is that Hibs have played their best football against Premiership teams this season. They are much more comfortable playing against teams who open out against them than they are in trying to break down packed defences.

The media are accusing Hibs of 'Hibsing it'. In other words, they are saying that Hibs have lost their bottle when it matters most. The outcome of the next two matches, a Scottish Cup quarter-final and a League Cup final, will go a long way to proving them right or wrong. One thing is for sure. If you are looking for your fans to invest in shares or buy tickets for a Scottish Cup tie or a League Cup Final, as Hibs are at the moment, it is not a good idea to lose three times in succession.

Alan Stubbs has revealed that his players exchanged strong words in the dressing room at Palmerston Park after losing to Queen of the South in midweek. That is good because it shows that they care. Stubbs also said that he sees no need to panic despite three consecutive defeats and stated that he will not be deterred by one bad week.

Falkirk have beaten Alloa 2–0 and are now two points ahead of Hibs, whose recent run of defeats is, not unexpectedly, proving costly. Ross County whom Hibs face in next week's League Cup Final have just lost 3–2 at home in the Scottish Cup to Dundee United. Former Hibs loanee Henri Anier scored two of United's goals. Hibs have sold 26,000 tickets for next week's final which given their recent form is excellent. If they can beat Inverness tomorrow, they will probably sell a few thousand more.

In January, Hibs signed an eighteen-year-old striker, Josh Peters, from a team from the Highlands called Strathspey Thistle. Peters has just scored a hat-trick in the Development Squad's 3–1 win over Dundee United. Maybe Alan Stubbs should play him against Inverness!

Hibs drew 1–1 with Inverness Caley Thistle. It was a game that they should have won. Caley played neat football but were extremely physical in their approach. James Keatings scored a fine goal after excellent work by Anthony Stokes, and David Gray and Liam Henderson missed great chances to add another. Caley came into the game late on and scored a superb equaliser so it's off to the Highlands for a replay in ten days' time. An extra game is the last thing Hibs need at the moment but the prize is a semi-final match against Dundee United. Rangers and Celtic will meet in the other semi.

Hibs are heading off to Malaga for a four-day break before next Sunday's League Cup final. They have played ten games in thirty-two days so they are more than ready for a rest and hopefully some sunshine. The performance against Inverness was much better than the form shown in recent league matches although Hibs again failed to take their chances and finish off a game they were controlling. Let's hope they can carry this improved form into the League Cup final. Alan Stubbs said last night that the players and staff will do everything they can to give the fans 'one unbelievable day next weekend'.

One player who probably won't be at Hampden is Dylan McGeouch who returned for the Scottish Cup tie but went off before the half-hour mark. Apparently it is the other side of his groin that is the problem this time. Dylan is richly talented but suffers more than his fair share of injuries. Since his arrival in the summer of 2014, he seems to have spent as much time on the treatment table as he has on the pitch. He has had surgery and scans and lots of rest and recuperation but still seems to break down regularly, which is a real concern going forward.

Hibs have arrived in the Costa del Sol. Here's hoping their four-day break does them good. Fraser Fyvie who hasn't played for several weeks is in the party and may come into contention for Hampden.

James Keatings has opened his heart after ending his sixteen-match goal drought yesterday. Keatings, who had never previously gone more than six games without scoring, revealed that he was so upset after missing an absolute sitter against Hearts in the last round that he didn't sleep that night. Hopefully the fine goal he scored yesterday will restore his confidence. We supporters get frustrated with players when they make mistakes and that is human nature but we should also remember that the players themselves are human and a poor performance, an error at a vital time, criticism from the fans or a combination of all of these can cause them great distress. When passions are running high, it's difficult for supporters to be objective and compassionate in their judgement. It is important that they try to see mistakes not just from the perspective of the impact they have on the team but also from the point of view of the effect such incidences have on the individual player who is at fault.

Hibs have continued their League Cup Final preparations in the Spanish Spring sunshine. Their training base in Malaga looks superb. Danny Carmichael and Dylan McGeouch are both out of the game with their ongoing groin injuries. Paul Hanlon is another absentee with his thigh tear.

Jason Cummings has been in bullish mood saying that he relishes the big occasions, that he has been visualising himself scoring in the final and that he would find it wonderful to stand on the pitch at Hampden at full time on Sunday and hear 'Sunshine on Leith' being played over the public address system.

Hibs have now left La Cala to fly home. Hopefully they are rested and raring to go for Sunday. Fraser Fyvie is just over five weeks into his recovery from a medial ligament injury. Knee knocks like that normally take six to eight weeks to heal so Hibs need to be careful not to rush him back too soon. Mind you they need him badly so hopefully he might be fit enough to take a place on the bench.

Hibs have now sold nearly 30,000 tickets, which is great. The referee for the League Cup final is Kevin Clancy.

John McGinn has been included in the Scotland squad for the upcoming international matches. He deserves his call up as he has had a tremendous season. John's form has shaded a bit lately so let's hope that on Sunday, buoyed by his first full international recognition, he plays the game of his life and inspires Hibs to victory.

The countdown towards Hampden has gathered momentum. Ivan Sproule, who played in Hibs' last League Cup win in 2007, had two spells at Easter Road and also spent time with Ross County. Ivan is thirty-five now and living back home in Belfast. He is making no secret of which of his former teams he will be supporting on Sunday. When Hibs beat Kilmarnock in the 2007 final, Ivan wore a green leprechaun hat as he and the rest of the team walked round Hampden to celebrate with the fans after the cup had been presented. He intends to be at Sunday's match supporting Hibs and wearing that very same hat. It would be nice if there is an identical outcome to last time.

If there is, there will be no victory parade on Sunday night. The police will be engaged in supervising the Scotland vs. France rugby international at Murrayfield earlier in the day and will therefore be unable to police a victorious Hibs homecoming (if the League Cup is won) at night. The Leader of City of Edinburgh Council said today that if Hibs do lift the trophy, the council will host a reception for the team on Monday 21 March. He suggested that a victory parade could then be held before the reception, which seems to make sense. All of this is hypothetical of course and Ross County may well have something to say about it.

There was a really good interview with Turnbull's Tornado and sweeper supreme John Blackley in the *Scotsman* newspaper. John played in three League Cup finals for Hibs and managed the club in another. He spoke about how his dad used to get too nervous to come and watch him playing but clearly felt immense pride in his performances and achievements. This was borne out when towards the end of his life, Mr Blackley told John, 'You've made this family's name son.' Very poignant indeed.

Fans from places as diverse as the United States, Afghanistan and Australia have travelled to Scotland to be at Hampden to support Hibs against Ross County. Let's hope that they have something to cheer about. Andy and Jamie Murray are playing in a tennis tournament in Indian Wells in California. They plan to set their alarms to 5am local time so that they can watch the final live via the Internet.

League Cup final day, and Margaret and I were on our way early. At the bus stop, we met up with some French rugby fans who were over for the international match with Scotland at Murrayfield. They wanted to know all about Hibs and they told us that they lived quite near Franck Sauzée.

As we were speaking, a van drove past. The driver opened his window, shouted '5–1' and made the dreaded, pathetic sign. Before I had a chance to respond with '7–0' or 'who knocked you out the Scottish Cup this year?', he was away. It would have been pretty childish if I had I suppose but I would have enjoyed it!

On the LRT bus up to the St Andrew Square bus station, there was a large group of Hibs fans all singing their hearts out even though it was only 9.30 in the morning. The John McGinn song seemed to be their favourite ditty. One of them said, 'The French people will be wondering what's going on. Do you think we should tell them that this is the party bus?'

When we arrived in Glasgow, we met up with our children – Patrick, Lisa, Dominic and Kevin – and three of our grandchildren – Roisin, Daniel and John – for brunch in the Counting

House on George Square. As always on these occasions, the pub was brimming with Hibees and the usual mixture of anticipation laced with apprehension was in the air. Once a few drinks had been consumed there was a bit of singing but it was obvious that no one was really hugely confident. Given our past experiences of 'Hibs at Hampden' that wasn't really surprising.

Inside Hampden, it was magnificent to look around and see the immense Hibs support which outnumbered the Ross County contingent by four to one. The match was like watching a Championship game over the last two seasons except that Ross County had better players than many of our second tier opponents.

County sat tight and defended in numbers. They were disciplined and resolute and worked incredibly hard. Hibs passed the ball well but overplayed when they got close to goal. In a first half of complete Hibs domination, Gary Woods, Ross County's reserve goalkeeper playing because their first choice Scott Fox was injured, made some good saves. Mark Oxley had nothing to do until County's first attack. Kevin Thomson gave the ball away carelessly in midfield and Michael Gardyne surged into a huge gap in the Hibs defence. Marvin Bartley tried to tackle him as Oxley raced from his goal. The ball broke clear for Gardyne to tap into the empty net. Hibs maintained their pressure and just before half time, Liam Fontaine seized upon a loose ball in the box following a Liam Henderson corner and drove the ball home.

Hibs again held the initiative in the second half but were unable to fashion or finish clear-cut chances. Anthony Stokes came closest with a neat turn and shot, which just shaved the post. Ross County's only effort of note was a chalked-off goal after Mark Oxley had been outjumped by Brian Graham for a high ball. Referee Kevin Clancy, who had a good game, decided that Oxley had been fouled. Television replays subsequently showed that he had been lucky!

In the ninetieth minute, with extra time looming, Hibs committed players forward again which was bold but not wise. The move broke down and County counterattacked at pace. The ball came across Hibs six-yard box and Liam Fontaine instead of using his weaker right foot to clear the ball as it came to him, tried to control it with his left foot. He was only able to knock it into the path of Alex Schalk who couldn't miss from two yards out.

So Hibs had lost at Hampden once again. It was distressing for me to watch my grandchildren crying their eyes out. In truth, I felt like doing the same myself. The players were distraught, none more so than John McGinn who was visibly upset. This was not a case of Hibs not turning up for a big match at the national stadium as has happened so often in the past. Just like against Falkirk in the semi-final last year, they played well, dominated the game and lost unluckily. It was heartbreaking.

One thing is crystal clear, though. Alan Stubbs has done a great job over the last couple of seasons but there is one problem he hasn't solved. Hibs control games but don't convert their chances. There is a lack of width due to Stubbs' preferred midfield diamond formation which prevents the team from creating enough clear-cut opportunities. When they do work an opening, their finishing is not sufficiently clinical. At the other end, the defenders switch off and concede avoidable goals. The fact that the goalkeeper is not sufficiently commanding contributes to this. All of the above has been evident in league games, in the play-off semi-final against Rangers last season and in our last two visits to Hampden. Missing chances and giving away soft goals is becoming a costly habit and Stubbs has to do something about it.

Alan Stubbs' post-match interview made for an interesting watch. Usually confident and positive, he was uncharacteristically downbeat. His state of mind was summed up when the interviewer put it to him that Wednesday's Scottish Cup replay at Inverness would provide the perfect opportunity for Hibs to get back on the rails. Stubbs replied, 'You're probably right but I can't think about that just now, the emotion is still too raw.' That said it all.

Jason Cummings described the feeling that the players experienced at full time as like 'being relegated all over again'. It felt exactly the same for the fans Jason! Liam Fontaine has apologised for his match-costing error. He gave his all in the game and played well apart from his crucial, costly mistake. He said that he felt even worse afterwards because he loves the club so much.

Alan Stubbs has been speaking again and his mood has noticeably lifted. He said that he had received a text from Martin Woods of Ross County, whom he had played with at Everton, telling him that Hibs had deserved to win Sunday's final. He also listed Hibs' progress since he took over as manager – League Cup quarter-final, Scottish Cup semi-final and second place in the Championship last season and League Cup final, Scottish Cup quarter-final so far and third in the Championship this season. As Stubbs said with a smile, 'It's hardly a disaster so we shouldn't be too hard on ourselves.' He's absolutely right of course but gallant failure needs to turn to success some time soon.

A newspaper article today revealed that Hibs had played in twenty-three major cup finals since their formation and had only won five of them. This is the worst finals record in Scottish football apart from Dumbarton who lost five out of six finals in the nineteenth century. Despite this record, Hibs fans stand by their club as Sunday's 30,000 strong support showed.

Alan Stubbs has also defended Liam Fontaine and Anthony Stokes. He described Fontaine's post-match apology as 'classy' and refused to point the finger at Stokes for Hibs' decline since he came into the team (only three wins in nine games). Stubbs said that Stokes has been improving his match sharpness all the time and that he would rather have him at his best at the business end of the season than now. There's no arguing with that point of view.

Three days after the League Cup final, Hibs have to play their quarter-final replay against Inverness in the Highland capital. It is a very quick turnaround after Sunday's strenuous efforts especially given the physicality of John Hughes' team and it will be a very difficult game to come through. It may be that it is time to introduce some fresh legs. Martin Boyle, James Keatings and Chris Dagnall all come to mind in that regard.

Hibs have achieved a great win at Inverness. Alan Stubbs resisted calls for changes and made only one alteration to the team, which lost unluckily to Ross County in the League Cup final. Kevin Thomson dropped out and James Keatings came in.

Hibs won 2–1 after two first half goals from Anthony Stokes who answered his critics by doing what he does best – putting the ball in the back of the net. Inverness pulled a goal back with thirteen minutes to go and after that the game became frantic with both teams missing a number of good chances. Mark Oxley who had been characteristically statuesque when Inverness Caledonian Thistle scored then took centre stage. First he was booked for time wasting when he claimed that he was trying to draw the referee's attention to the fact that he had lost his contact lens, which was certainly how it looked to me. Then he had to go off to be replaced by Otso Virtanen who was making his debut. Referee Steven Finnie contrived to find seven minutes of additional time but Hibs, despite a nervous moment or two from Virtanen, managed to hold on for a famous victory, which was all the more creditable for coming hard on the heels of Sunday's gruelling and disappointing cup final. Oxley was also booked for time wasting against Hearts in the last round so he will miss the semi-final against Dundee United.

Last night's result and performance was one in the eye for the national press and media who have been quick to condemn Hibs after the disappointment against Ross County. It wasn't that Hibs didn't turn up at Hampden. They most certainly did. It was just that they came up with their usual mix of missed chances and carelessly conceded goals.

Even though they won last night, there was still an element of carelessness in both Hibs finishing and, at times, defending. They really must eradicate these twin failings when they travel to Kirkcaldy to play Raith Rovers at the weekend.

It's not all doom and gloom, though. Hibs have reached the Scottish Cup semi-final for the second successive season. Alan Stubbs' record in cup competitions has been outstanding. The feeling grows that this could be Hibs year in the 'Scottish'. Just how wonderful would that be?

For the moment though it's back to the bread and butter of league business. Hibs will travel to Kirkcaldy knowing that Falkirk have just beaten Rangers 3–2. Rangers led 2–0 with nineteen minutes to go so it was an amazing comeback by a

Falkirk team that just never gives up. It is very bad news for Hibs and makes victory at Stark's Park absolutely essential.

Hibs have lost their fourth consecutive league match. Anthony Stokes gave Hibs the lead in the first half but weak defending and profligate finishing (the usual mixture) allowed Raith Rovers to score twice and win the game. Rovers, on their tight, bumpy pitch were everything you would expect – big and physical, totally committed and full of hunger for the fight. Hibs were lacklustre yet still had enough chances to win comfortably. The best fell to Jason Cummings who, from two yards out and faced with an empty net, contrived to hit the ball against the underside of the cross bar.

Alan Stubbs has backed his players loyally since he became Hibs manager. It seems like the surrender at Stark's Park was the last straw for him though. He was visibly angry post-match and spoke of his team 'not performing' and 'making basic mistakes' and stated that some players were in danger of being dropped. I am sure that Jason Cummings comes into that category. He hasn't scored for eight games and missed a sitter on Saturday. To be fair to Jason, the ball bobbled as it came to him but he was only two yards out and an empty net was gaping in front of him. He should have been able to get his body over the ball, keep it down and guide it into the net.

There is now a two-week hiatus due to Scotland playing international friendly matches. Usually I can't be bothered with international games, finding them a boring distraction from the business of watching Hibs. This time I am glad that Hibs are going to get a break. The players need it. They have played an awful lot of games and need a rest. Hopefully, too, when fixtures resume with a league match at St Mirren at the beginning of April, Paul Hanlon, Danny Carmichael, Dylan

McGeouch and Fraser Fyvie will all be fit again or, at worst, close to full fitness.

Lewis Stevenson and Darren McGregor have been having their say about Hibs' recent demise. Lewis says that the team hasn't played well since Christmas, which is true. He feels that initially he and his colleagues were continuing to get results and that this masked the fact that their performance levels had dropped. Now performances are still below par and the results are going against the team. Lewis speaks as he plays – straight from the heart.

Darren very honestly stated that for a team of Hibs' stature to lose four league games in a row is just not acceptable. He thinks that the supporters deserve better (hear! hear!) and is confident that results will improve after the international break. All of those same supporters very much hope that he is right.

John McGinn has joined up with Scotland ahead of their friendly match with Denmark. In an interview with the BBC, he seemed more concerned with Hibs' current form than with the prospect of making his full international debut. In admitting that his personal performances had shaded since the turn of the year, John made it clear that all the Hibs players are very keen to get their season back on track.

Yesterday, Danny Handling played his first game for Hibs since incurring a cruciate ligament injury last July. He played the first half in a 1-0 win for the Development Squad against St Mirren. With so many midfield players currently injured, it is good to have Handling back. I think Danny is a talented player but in his first team outings to date, he hasn't done himself full justice. There would be no better time than now for him to start doing exactly that.

I have just finished reading former Hibs player David Farrell's book *Taxi for Farrell* in which he lays bare the life of the journeyman footballer. It is an excellent read and very well written. I thoroughly enjoyed it. Farrell spent seven and a half years at Hibs mainly as a midfield warhorse during Alex Miller's time as manager. Always fearless and completely committed, he complemented the more skilful players like Darren Jackson, Michael O'Neill and Kevin McAllister. Farrell is now Alex Rae's assistant manager at St Mirren.

Easter Sunday has come early this year and it has been a very pleasant family day. After mass this morning, all the family gathered at my daughter Lisa's. We exchanged Easter Eggs and tucked into a sumptuous brunch provided by Lisa and her husband Derrick. We had a choice of bacon, egg, sausage or black pudding on rolls followed by chocolate cake or a Victoria sponge. Inevitably the conversation turned to football and Hibs. Falkirk have just lost at home to Livingston which was a real bonus for Hibs. Loanee Sam Stanton put Livingston two goals up in the ninetieth minute to do his parent club a real favour but this indomitable Falkirk team wasn't finished yet. Will Vaulks pulled a goal back in the ninety-first minute and then the Bairns won a ninety-third minute penalty. Thankfully the normally prolific John Baird missed from the spot. Falkirk have only lost four league games this season and, to state the obvious, they are very hard to beat. They are still six points ahead of Hibs, who now have three games in hand.

Raith Rovers have chalked up their third consecutive single goal victory in a week and are now only four points behind Hibs. The Scottish Championship is a tough, unforgiving league. Hibs have eight games to play. There are home matches against Livingston, Falkirk, Dumbarton, Rangers and Queen of the

South and trips to St Mirren, Morton and Alloa. None of these matches, which start with a trip to Paisley, will be easy.

Jason Cummings seems to be getting over his barely credible miss against Raith Rovers. He is currently on Scotland Under 21 duty and claims that his confidence hasn't been affected at all. He has explained his miss at Stark's Park by saying that it was due to the bobbly pitch. He is putting the blame firmly on the Raith groundsman. There is something in what he says as the ball did bounce up unevenly as it came to him but he certainly should have scored.

Hibs need Jason back in scoring form as soon as possible. Mind you, I am not sure that Alan Stubbs will even start him against St Mirren. I think that he might go for a front pairing of Anthony Stokes and James Keatings. Stokes is back in the goals and Keatings scored a hat-trick the last time Hibs visited Paisley.

Yesterday was a good day on the international front for Jason Cummings and John McGinn.

Jason scored twice for Scotland Under 21s as they beat Ireland 3–1 in Paisley. He didn't start the game well missing a penalty and a couple of chances and his body language betrayed low confidence but, Jason being Jason, he kept going and got his reward with two trademark close-range finishes. This will get him in the right frame of mind for Saturday when he returns to St Mirren's ground although as I said earlier I am not certain that he will start the game. His timely international brace will have certainly helped his chances though.

John played for the full Scotland team against Denmark at Hampden and was named Man of the Match in a 1–0 victory. This will put him in a good frame of mind as Hibs embark on a crucial and congested Championship run in. John's form has shaded in recent weeks and it would be great to have him back to his best for the final part of the season. Mind you, he played the whole match at Hampden, which won't do a lot for his freshness factor.

Hibs have signed a twenty-nine-year-old Irish goalkeeper called Conrad Logan. Logan was on Leicester City's books for fifteen years, which suggests that he has something to offer. On the other hand, he spent a large part of these years on loan to lower league clubs and has been without a team since being released last summer. He has apparently been recovering from a serious Achilles tendon injury. Alan Stubbs is clearly concerned about the fact that Mark Oxley is unavailable for the Scottish Cup semi-final with Dundee United through suspension. He obviously doesn't fully trust Oxley's understudy Otso Virtanen, which is interesting considering that he signed him on a three-and-a-half-year contract.

Alan Stubbs has given his first interviews since the defeat to Raith Rovers almost two weeks ago. He was fairly low key but made a point of urging his players to end the season on a high. There is absolutely no doubt that that is exactly what they have to do. The team will be helped by the return of Paul Hanlon who is back in full training but none of Fraser Fyvie, Dylan McGeouch or Danny Carmichael is ready to return yet which is disappointing.

April 2016

The Polar Bear and the Penalties

Disaster at Alloa – fatal four minutes against Falkirk – Logan's semi-final heroics – victory over Rangers – battling for second spot

Hibs have returned to action after a fortnight's break with a disappointing 2–2 draw against St Mirren in Paisley. Both Liam Fontaine and James Keatings had joined the injury list so the squad was further depleted. Fortunately, Paul Hanlon who has been badly missed was fit enough to return to central defence.

Hibs went ahead when Jason Cummings scored his third goal in Paisley in a week with a cool finish after a pinpoint pass from John McGinn. Saints equalised when Rocco Quinn, who looked well offside, was allowed to carry on and knock the ball past Mark Oxley. Hibs protested furiously but all their complaints fell on deaf ears.

Worse was to follow when slack defending allowed Lawrence Shankland to put the Buddies ahead. Alan Stubbs really went for it at this point and Hibs ended the match with four strikers on the pitch. One of them, Farid El Alagui fired home an eighty-ninth-minute equaliser after good work by Anthony Stokes.

Around the time that Farid was scoring, Queen of the South were drawing level with Falkirk and Raith Rovers were pulling back to 3–3 with Rangers so all three top Championship sides drew today – a case for Hibs of nothing lost and nothing gained.

Hibs have now taken just one point from their last five league matches, which is a totally unacceptable return. Both Hibs and Rangers have matches in midweek. Hibs are at home to Livingston and Rangers entertain Dumbarton. If Rangers win, they will be crowned winners of the Scottish Championship and will be automatically promoted. For much of the season, Hibs posed a serious challenge to Rangers but they have fallen away in inexplicable fashion in recent weeks. It can only be down to a combination of fatigue due to all the extra cup matches they have had to play and the continuing, costly habit of dominating games but failing to win them.

Alan Stubbs looked ahead to the match on Hibs TV yesterday and he was very downbeat as he has increasingly been since the team's run without a win has developed. His previous infectious confidence and total belief have not been in evidence. Maybe, like we fans, he is beginning to feel the pressure. If that is the case, it is hardly surprising. The Livingston game will be Hibs' first home fixture since they met Inverness in the Scottish Cup in early March.

Writing in his regular weekly column in Monday's *Edinburgh Evening News*, Mickey Weir who is always supportive of the club, did nothing to relieve that pressure. He stated quite unequivocally that it was time for the players to 'show character and snap out of their slump'. He added that nothing less than six points from the next two games against Livingston and Alloa would be acceptable. In my opinion, he is entirely right.

Hibs have at last got back to winning ways by beating Livingston 2–1. It was tough, though. Livingston, who are fighting to avoid relegation, were very well organised and tremendously resolute. Their work rate was immense and their manager, David Hopkin, clearly knows what he is doing.

Livi scored first after Hibs (yes you've guessed it) failed to clear their lines. With the crowd becoming increasingly anxious and impatient, it took Hibs until the seventy-fifth minute to score. Then came two great goals in three minutes. First, a clever flick from Jason Cummings set up Anthony Stokes to fire home from the edge of the box. Then Martin Boyle, on as a substitute, latched on to a Livingston clearance to rifle home a brilliant volley from all of thirty yards. Alan Stubbs said after the game that he had told the players at half time to keep believing in themselves. I think that that was good advice. Stubbs also described Boyle's goal as a 'special strike'. It most certainly was.

Recently Hibs have advertised the following: new season tickets, a second share issue, mascot packages, corporate hospitality, stadium tours and tickets for the Player of the Year dinner. This non-stop barrage of commercial 'opportunities' is understandable as the club needs to maximise its income but when the team is struggling as it has been doing recently, I think Hibs should ease off a little on the relentless plugging of such ventures.

John Doolan has fronted Hibs weekly press conference as Alan Stubbs had decided to take a back seat. Doolan spoke well (he always does) and made his views on Saturday's trip to Alloa clear. When it was put to him that Alloa's plastic playing surface is notoriously difficult particularly since they narrowed their pitch to curb other teams' creativity, he responded by saying that Hibs had to go there and win, and that there could be no excuses made. I liked that. Doolan, by the way, made no reference to the Chuckle Brothers.

I liked Martin Boyle's modesty too. He has described his wonder goal against Livingston as a 'fluke'. He is being hard on himself. His strike was superb and he should learn from it. He is not the best of finishers when he has time to think but can score impressively when he reacts instinctively. He scored a fine goal at Falkirk last season when he let fly without weighing up his options or hesitating as he sometimes does. Go for it Martin. When you have a chance, don't think about it just shoot. Then we'll see even more goals from you.

Ridiculously and unforgivably, Hibs who should be stretching every sinew to avoid having to spend a third consecutive season in the Scottish Championship have gone to already relegated Alloa who hadn't won at home all season and lost 1–0.

An extremely lacklustre performance saw Hibs barely create a chance. Alloa's goal, just like the one awarded to St Mirren last week, was highly contentious but really that is not the point. Hibs should be putting three or four goals past Alloa. They have now lost not just to Alloa this season but to Morton, Raith Rovers, Queen of the South and Dumbarton (twice!). It just isn't good enough and Hibs' collapse since beating Hearts in the Scottish Cup is totally bewildering. Falkirk and Raith both won again so Hibs could now conceivably finish fourth in the league, which would be an insult to their magnificently loyal supporters.

Hibs play Falkirk at Easter Road in midweek in the ultimate of the many must-win games they have had this season. Watching

Alan Stubbs post-match interview from Alloa today makes me wonder if he will be able to inspire his team to get back to their best for this crucial match. When asked if Hibs could bounce back against Falkirk, Stubbs replied, 'They have to respond because Alloa was not good enough.' He said this in the most downbeat of fashions and he looked and sounded like a man who had seen his Plan A cease to work and wasn't sure what his Plan B should be.

We shouldn't underestimate Stubbs though. For all Hibs' recent disappointing form, he has done an excellent job since arriving at Easter Road and he strikes me as being a winner.

Interestingly, there has been no news as yet of Hibs persuading Paul Hanlon to sign a new contract. Hanlon's current deal runs out in the summer. Paul has his moments in games when he switches off or allows himself to be outmuscled by the striker he is marking but these moments are much less frequent than they used to be and he is an excellent central defender who has served our club very well indeed. Surely it is a no brainer to offer him another contract? Are Hibs waiting to see what league they will be in next season or has Hanlon told them that he intends to seek pastures new? As of yet, there is no hint as to which of these scenarios is the more likely. We will just have to wait and see.

The Brack family have bought their season tickets for season 2016–17. We love our team and stand by our club even if, at times, it can drive its supporters mad. The lows (and Hibs fans suffer their fair share of them) just make the highs all the more enjoyable when they come along.

The coverage of the ignominious defeat to Alloa in tonight's *Edinburgh Evening News* makes for interesting reading. Mickey

Weir in his column says that Hibs' season is at its lowest ebb. He also says that he reckons Hibs' recent dreadful league form has come from complacency engendered by success against Premier League clubs in the League Cup and Scottish Cup. David Hardie, who has covered Hibs fortunes in the *Evening News* for as long as I can remember, described the team's performance at the Indodrill Stadium as 'woeful'.

Usually the local journalist will choose his words carefully as he has to maintain a good relationship with the club and, in particular, the manager. For David to express himself in such strong terms shows just how bad Hibs were against Alloa.

Alan Stubbs is coming under pressure on the fans' websites. I think it's totally unfair to be questioning the manager's position given how well he had done up until the last couple of months. There is no doubt though that Hibs' decline has been as swift and significant as it has been unexpected. Two months ago Stubbs was being strongly tipped to be the next Celtic manager. Such speculation has long since ceased.

Still though, our manager stands by his players. He has stated in a number of interviews that he has total trust and confidence in them. It is not clear what it is in recent performances and results which gives him that level of belief in players who have managed to take only four points out of the last twenty-one available to them in the second tier of Scottish football.

So now Hibs take on Peter Houston's highly impressive Falkirk side in a game that could not be any more important to the outcome of their season. Falkirk have good players. They are consistent, disciplined, well organised and stay in games from the first whistle to the last often winning like they did last Saturday with late goals.

They know how to play against Hibs. They will defend in depth and hit on the counter attack. With the exception of Rangers every team in the league plays like that against Hibs and it works for them.

Hibs have been losing consistently to teams with far fewer resources than they have. These teams' players are inferior to those at Easter Road but still they beat Hibs. They do so because they display complete commitment and concentration, take their chances and keep their back door closed. If you look at the statistics published after matches, the information on Hibs games is consistent. They dominate possession, have far more attempts on goal and win significantly more corners but, as often as not, fail to win. It is just not good enough. It has to change.

Hibs have held their Player of the Year dinner. The awards have been won by Paul Hanlon (Moment of the Season – his last-minute, equalising goal at Tynecastle), Liam Henderson (Young Player of the Season) and John McGinn (Player of the Season).

Personally I think that Jason Cummings deserves the Young Player award for scoring twenty-one goals so far this season. John McGinn was brilliant until the League Cup semi-final against St Johnstone in January. His form has really shaded off since then. There would be no better time for him to recapture his best form than in the crucial weeks between now and the end of the season.

Just when we thought that things couldn't get any worse on the Hibs front, they have done exactly that. Hibs were leading

Falkirk 2–0 with four minutes to go and Falkirk had been reduced to ten men when Aaron Muirhead was sent off with quarter of an hour left.

Falkirk won a free kick just inside Hibs' half. David McCracken – the Falkirk centre half who had gifted Jason Cummings Hibs' first goal with a misdirected header back to his goalkeeper and conceded the penalty from which Cummings had scored the second goal – made his way forward. At this pivotal point in their season, Hibs contrived to leave McCracken unmarked and when the ball came into the box, he headed it into the net. McCracken's determination to atone for his errors personified the indomitability of Peter Houston's side. They came again in the ninetieth minute and won a throw on the right touchline. Will Vaulks hurled the ball long into the penalty area, Falkirk won the flick on at the near post and while Niklas Gunnarsson switched off at the back post, Bob McHugh eluded him to head home a barely deserved equaliser.

Hibs' chances of finishing second in the Championship are now very slim indeed. They weren't brilliant against the Bairns but they certainly did enough to win the game. Where Falkirk, who are strong physically and mentally and play to the last whistle, kept going, Hibs, just like they did in the League Cup Final against Ross County, displayed a carelessness in game management which cost them dearly. It was a draw which felt like a defeat and a total sickener for the faithful Hibs supporters who had turned up in numbers once again on a miserably wet night.

Alan Stubbs attempted to be upbeat after the game saying that there had been many positives in Hibs performance in the first eighty-five minutes of the game. There were some but not as many as he claimed. He then dismissed the catastrophic end to the match as 'two lapses in concentration'. They were certainly that and of a major variety. The best part of two seasons in charge should have been enough time for Stubbs to inculcate an ability to concentrate at crucial moments into his players.

One fan tonight has posted the following message, 'I am going to ask Hibs to lower my coffin when I die so they can let me down one last time.' Gallows humour, of course, but you can see exactly where he is coming from.

Leeann Dempster has publicly backed Alan Stubbs and she is right to have done so. She said that he hasn't become a bad manager over-night and that he and his management team will be at Easter Road on a long-term basis. Let's hope that she is right on both counts.

I have just brought myself to watch the highlights of last night's game. For the first Falkirk goal, Darren McGregor switched off and allowed David McCracken a free header which, it has to be said, he bulleted home in convincing style.

For the second goal, Lee Miller out-jumped Lewis Stevenson to flick the ball on. Bob McHugh reacted sharply. Niklas Gunnarsson didn't react at all. The question has to be asked – why was one of Hibs' smaller players in Stevenson marking Miller rather than Paul Hanlon or Darren McGregor?

The press and media, particularly the sections of it with a West coast bias, are having a field day. They are again accusing Hibs of 'Hibsing it' after the late capitulation against Falkirk. I don't agree at all. Hibs have been careless at the back and profligate in front of the opposition's goal but they have never lacked fight or bottle in any game.

Dundee United now lie in wait in the Scottish Cup semi-final and this time only 12,500 Hibs fans will be travelling to the national stadium which is quite a contrast to the 30,000 or so who went west in hope of seeing Hibs triumph in the League Cup Final against Ross County just one short month ago. The Bracks will be out in force. Sons Patrick and Dominic, daughter Lisa and grandchildren Roisin, Daniel and John will join Margaret and me at the game.

Jason Cummings has been speaking without thinking again. He has referred to Hibs' defeat of Dundee United in the League Cup earlier in the season as a 'drubbing' and has said that United will be 'wary of getting another drubbing'. It sounds to me like he is doing a good job of firing up the opposition.

Hibs have won their way to the Scottish Cup final for the third time in five seasons. They beat Dundee United in a dramatic penalty shootout with the hero being goalkeeper Conrad Logan. Big Conrad, whose nickname is 'The Polar Bear', was only playing because Mark Oxley was suspended but for the first time since Ben Williams left it looked like Hibs had a proper goalkeeper between the posts. Logan hadn't played for sixteen months after rupturing his Achilles tendon in December 2014 but you would never have known it.

He was only able to start jogging again in January of this year and Alan Stubbs' decision to take him on until the end of the season to cover for Oxley has proved a masterstroke. Conrad is a big lad and his inability to train for a long period won't have helped his body shape. He may look bulky but his agility belied his build. Four times in the match he denied United forwards who were through on him one on one. He also communicated and organised his defence throughout the game.

Hibs should have won the match in normal time but as ever they didn't turn early dominance into goals. Jason Cummings even missed a penalty in the most ridiculous way. He attempted to do a 'Panenka' and made a complete hash of it, chipping the ball over the bar. It was all about his ego and not at all about the good of the team. When you get a penalty in a Scottish Cup semi-final, you concentrate on putting it away and on nothing else. Cummings' vain decision to try to impress by producing a piece of risky flamboyance did not endear him to the Hibs support.

By extra time, Hibs were out on their feet. The large number of games that the team has had to play was, unsurprisingly, definitely having an effect on the players' energy levels with John McGinn and Liam Henderson looking particularly tired. In the end, Hibs were happy to go to penalties. At this point, big Conrad, who had already performed admirably, raised his game to an even higher level.

The Polar Bear was ice cool as he saved first from Blair Spittal and then from Billy McKay. United only managed to get on the score sheet with their third and fourth penalties. By this time, Hibs, who had gone second in the shootout, had already scored three goals with John McGinn, Paul Hanlon and Martin Boyle all having kept their nerve to dispatch excellent spot kicks. This left Jason Cummings to come forward to take Hibs fourth kick and redeem himself for his earlier self-indulgence. He did exactly that by placing the ball low to the goalkeeper's right to seal a 4–2 penalty shootout win for Hibs. Cue an eruption of euphoria among the Hibs support and a spirited rendition of 'Sunshine on Leith' before everyone headed for the happiest of journeys home. Having lost to Alloa last Saturday and thrown away a two-goal lead in the space of the final four minutes against Falkirk on Tuesday, it was good to end what hadn't been the best of weeks on a high note.

It has been interesting to watch the post-match interviews. Conrad Logan came across really well. The big man from

Donegal was modest and pleasant. He said that he had always had a good record for saving penalties and had fully expected to save one or two of the spot kicks. He did exactly that. One journalist had written that Conrad looked like a 'Sunday League goalkeeper'. Well, he certainly didn't perform like one. If you have had a serious injury and been unable to train fully for over a year, you are not going to be in your best shape, are you? What Logan clearly is though is an experienced goalkeeper who brings organisation and composure to his defence which, at the moment, is exactly what Hibs need.

Hibs play Rangers at Easter Road in midweek as their unrelenting schedule continues and, in my opinion and that of many other Hibees, Conrad Logan should be in goal. More than likely, though, Alan Stubbs will stand by his man and choose Mark Oxley.

Stubbs went easy on Jason Cummings in his post-match interview. Obviously happy and relieved to have won, he contented himself with describing Cummings as 'some boy'. I really like Jason. He gives it everything and, although still an erratic finisher, he scores an awful lot of goals and has, I think, a really good future ahead of him. At times though his self-confidence crosses the line into arrogance and egotism and he says and does things that are not the wisest. His failed 'Panenka' was a case in point. I wouldn't have called Jason Cummings 'some boy'. I would have said that he was a very lucky boy that his piece of nonsense didn't deprive his club, his teammates and his supporters of a place in the Scottish Cup final.

Hibs are indeed in the Scottish Cup final and I have had a growing feeling all season that this might be the year in which we finally lay our hoodoo in the 'Scottish' to rest. Hibs' recent form has been unconvincing and the players are very tired after the most exhausting of seasons but they have been at their best in cup competitions, which is a very good sign indeed.

Rangers have beaten Celtic on penalties to win the second Scottish Cup semi-final and it is they who will play Hibs in the final on Saturday 21 May. In the five weeks until then, Hibs face a series of crucial league matches starting with the visit of Mark Warburton's truly transformed Ibrox outfit on Wednesday night. Hibs must focus on the league now and forget the Scottish Cup for the foreseeable future.

Hibs require three points from every game and need to fully use their pool of players to avoid already tired key players becoming even more fatigued as they approach the promotion play-offs. There are some exciting and nerve wracking times ahead.

Conrad Logan has just celebrated his thirtieth birthday. The media coverage since Saturday's star performance by the man who now seems to go by the soubriquet 'The Bear' has been generous to his goalkeeping but less complimentary about his physique. I couldn't care less if Conrad is carrying a few extra pounds. Regular training and participation in matches will soon take care of that.

The big Donegal man does a nice line in self-deprecation. Describing how he had phoned home to his family after Saturday's match to discuss his moment of glory, Conrad said that his daughter who had watched the game on television along with the rest of the family asked him why he had dived the wrong way for one of the penalties. A bit harsh on a man whose goalkeeping excellence was there for all to see.

One man who may not have been over-impressed is Alan Stubbs. Hibs' manager has already stated that he will select Mark Oxley for the vital midweek match with Rangers at Easter Road. I think that is very unfair on Logan. Stubbs' high regard for Oxley as a goalkeeper is something that I and many other fans do not share. He is far too easily beaten, makes regular errors and does not command his area. Big Mark is popular with his teammates and seems to have really bought into Hibs ethos. With his height and agility, he should be a top goalkeeper but whether it is due to a lack of self-belief or an inability to maintain concentration, he has, in my opinion, never performed consistently in his time at Easter Road.

The build up to the Hibs vs. Rangers game has not been boring. Alan Stubbs has made it clear that Hibs will not provide a guard of honour for the newly crowned League Champions. He says that he telephoned Mark Warburton to congratulate him and that that will suffice. He doesn't consider his decision to be disrespectful.

Marvin Bartley who played really well at Hampden on Saturday was asked what he made of Rangers' victory over Celtic on Sunday. He replied that he hadn't seen the Old Firm game as he had decided to watch the *Antiques Roadshow*, which was on another channel at the same time.

James Keatings was on Twitter before Rangers and Celtic played declaring his support for Celtic. His tweet included the entreaty, 'Come on the Hoops'.

I think that all of this will just fire Rangers up tonight and that is something Hibs should be looking to avoid. Keatings should show more respect for his own club's supporters and focus his energy on improving his own performances, which have, of late, had plenty scope for said improvement. When he is on form, though, Keats is an excellent striker. A return to his early season form would be most welcome.

Talking of Celtic, their manager Ronny Deila has announced that he will step down at the end of the season. He has simply jumped before he was pushed. His was a cheap option appointment and his reign has been distinctly underwhelming.

His team selections have constantly raised questions. He signed the precocious Ryan Christie from Inverness but has never picked him to start a game. Even more bewilderingly, having snatched Scott Allan from Hibs grasp, he has rarely played him. When you think of how much ability Allan has that just doesn't make any sense at all.

Hibs have beaten Rangers 3–2 in a pulsating match at Easter Road. Rangers dominated possession and passed the ball superbly throughout. They lacked a cutting edge in attack though and Hibs posed them constant problems on the break.

Alan Stubbs went with a 3-5-2 formation and when Rangers were on the attack, Hibs usually had nine men behind the ball. For all their possession, Rangers found it hard to create clear openings and when Hibs counter attacked Jason Cummings and Anthony Stokes were always a threat.

Cummings put Hibs ahead with a fine early strike. He has now scored eight goals against Rangers in the last two seasons. Stokes added a second when his right wing cross was palmed into his own net by Wes Foderingham in the Rangers goal.

As half time approached, Hibs were looking reasonably comfortable only for Mark Oxley to make a complete mess of a misdirected cross from James Tavernier to gift Jason Holt the simplest of finishes.

Rangers controlled possession in the second half but Niklas Gunnarsson rifled in a superb volley following a John McGinn corner and Hibs were two in front again. As the clock ticked down, Oxley was beaten again by a Barrie Mackay strike from distance. He then conceded a totally unnecessary corner in the dying seconds. To his credit, though, he came out decisively and caught the ball superbly when the corner came over and Hibs had secured what could be a crucial three points.

After the game, Alan Stubbs refused to criticise Oxley. The press and media didn't hold back, though, and he was roundly taken to task for yet another unconvincing display. The fans made their feelings clear during the second half when Conrad Logan emerged to do a warm up jog. The Hibs support rose as one to accord him a standing ovation. I have sympathy for Oxley because he doesn't make his mistakes on purpose and will be feeling bad after his performance against Rangers. I think that it is time for Conrad Logan to become Hibs' regular number one though.

The Rangers game was a very tense occasion. Rangers enjoyed 69% of the possession and Hibs had to work tirelessly and concentrate completely to keep them at bay. It was a nerve-wracking watch, though. My youngest son Kevin's secretary was at the game with her sister. She said that she was so uptight throughout the game that she had to go to the pub after the game and have three brandies to calm herself down. I know how she feels – every match this season has had a must-win feel to it and almost every game has had a close outcome. It ensures that spectating is never a relaxing experience.

Hibs put a tremendous amount of effort into beating Rangers after going to extra time on Saturday and must be feeling fatigue as they go into the weekend's visit to Morton. Alan Stubbs doesn't think so though. He said that Hibs are now 'immune' to tiredness. I very much hope that he is right.

John McGinn who was back to his best last night and the predatory Jason Cummings have been nominated for the award of

Scottish Championship Player of the Year. They both deserve it. Their rivals are Lee Wallace and Martyn Waghorn of Rangers. It would be nice to see John or Jason follow in Scott Allan's footsteps from last season and win the award.

Hibs' relentless schedule of games continues. The visit to Morton will be their third punishing match in seven days. Morton meanwhile have been resting for a week. When Morton shocked Hibs 3–0 at Easter Road and set in motion the collapse in form which has cost Hibs so dearly in respect of their promotion prospects, they played a high-octane game. They pressed non-stop, ran themselves into the ground and were pacey and sharp on the break. They really knocked Hibs out of their stride and, in all honesty, the final margin could have been more than three goals. I expect a similar Morton performance today.

Jim Duffy seems able to really motivate his team for matches against the club that sacked him as manager in 1998. He possibly still resents losing his job (not that he should, because his dismissal was fully deserved) and it may be that he channels that resentment into seeking revenge when he comes up against Hibs.

Falkirk next visit Raith Rovers. Hibs fans will be desperately hoping that Raith can pull off a win. Mind you, if Hibs had beaten Alloa two weeks ago (I still can't believe that Hibs could lose that game) and held their 2–0 lead against Falkirk for just four minutes more rather than capitulating defensively , they would very much be in pole position in the race for second place. Second place would, of course, have brought with it the extra ten days recuperation time that comes with attaining that position in the league. Now Hibs have to keep winning games against difficult teams while suffering from the effects of a gruelling programme of fixtures and hope that Falkirk slip up in one or both of the final two matches to gain that much needed period in which to recharge their batteries.

Hibs have had yet another disappointing Championship day. Morton held Hibs to a 0–0 draw at Cappielow. Alan Stubbs gave John McGinn the break he very much needed and replaced him with Liam Henderson. Surprisingly, given the fatigue levels within the team, he didn't make any other changes. Henderson lobbed over when clean through and Jason Cummings had a goal questionably ruled out for offside. That was really the sum total of Hibs' attacking efforts. Falkirk drew 2–2 with Raith in Kirkcaldy. Yet again, the Bairns found a late equaliser.

Hibs now need to win their last two games and hope that Falkirk slip up at home to Morton next Sunday, which I don't think is very likely. Alternatively, Hibs have to score goals galore in their last two games against Dumbarton and Queen of the South to overhaul Falkirk's seven-goal advantage in goal difference. Given the fact that Hibs are finding it hard to play with urgency and are running on empty, I don't consider that to be a likely scenario either.

Only three days on from their last match with Morton, Hibs' tired legs are about to go into action again. Dumbarton are the visitors to Easter Road and their manager, Stevie Aitken, is seeking his third win over Hibs this season. That just should not be allowed to happen. Hibs need to win well and to score as many goals as possible. No matter how tired they are, they just have to prove themselves to be too good for Dumbarton in a game as vital as this one.

Alan Stubbs has said that he thinks that the pressure to finish second is now all on Falkirk. I am really not sure how he has managed to come to that conclusion. He did have some good news on the injury front though as Liam Fontaine is back in the squad and Dylan McGeouch and Danny Carmichael are close to a return. Christian Nade is Dumbarton's only doubt for the game. Let's hope he doesn't make it because the big ex-Hearts man always reserves his best performances for matches against Hibs.

Hibs have played really well to beat Dumbarton 4–0. In truth it was four going on seven. With more composed finishing, Hibs could even have notched double figures. Jamie Ewings, the Dumbarton goalkeeper, played his part in keeping the score reasonably respectable by making a string of outstanding saves. Alan Stubbs rested David Gray and Jason Cummings and gave Conrad Logan a start in goal. Cummings' replacement, James Keatings, scored twice in the first thirteen minutes and both his strikes were excellent finishes.

An own goal from Kevin Cawley, which Keatings was claiming was his, and a last minute counter from Anthony Stokes saw Hibs trim their goal difference deficit to three.

In all honesty, the goal difference deficit could have been wiped out entirely. Liam Henderson, Niklas Gunnarsson, Martin Boyle and Stokes all missed good chances. Lewis Stevenson hit the post with a fine shot.

After the game, Alan Stubbs professed himself well pleased with the final outcome saying to the interviewer, 'I would have bitten your hand off if you had offered me that score line before the game.' He must have known inside, though, that Hibs missed a great opportunity to take goal difference out of the equation going into Sunday's final round of Championship fixtures.

The Dumbarton manager Stevie Aitken, who has done a great job in keeping the Sons in the second tier, claimed post-match that his players had been exhausted after their match against St Mirren on Saturday. My response to that would be 'Try being Hibs!' I certainly didn't detect any signs of tiredness in Dumbarton's play.

They fought, harried and laid their bodies on the line right until the final whistle. They are a very experienced side and that showed in the way they wasted time and committed a number of cynical fouls. For once Christian Nade, who came on as a second half substitute and clearly wasn't fully fit, didn't score against Hibs. Nor did former Easter Road striker Paul Heffernan who replaced Nade up front and put in a committed shift. I always felt that Heffernan should have done better at Easter Road. He came nowhere near fulfilling his potential as a Hibs player.

The four nominations for Scotland's Manager of the Year are Mark Warburton at Rangers, Peter Houston at Falkirk, Jim McIntyre of Ross County and Jim McInally of Peterhead. I think Alan Stubbs is unlucky not to be nominated and would definitely have received a nomination if Hibs hadn't slumped so badly in the league in the last few months. However, the slump did take place and can't be ignored.

There were encouraging signs against Dumbarton and much more zip about the team's play. They can go into Sunday's season denouement when Hibs play Queen of the South and Morton travel to Falkirk with some hope of still achieving that vital second place finishing position.

Peter Houston had said before Hibs played Dumbarton that he hoped that Dumbarton wouldn't ease off because they had made themselves safe in the Championship for another season (they most certainly didn't, which I am sure was his purpose in making the remark). Alan Stubbs described Houston's comments as, 'Just Peter up to his old tricks again'.

John McGinn and Jason Cummings have been nominated to be Scotland's Young Player of the Year, which is their second recent nomination and greatly to their credit. McGinn meanwhile has said that he will stay with Hibs next season whether they are promoted or not which is even more to his credit. Martin Boyle's spellbinding strike against Livingston has been nominated for goal of the season. It will take something special to beat it.

If Hibs and Falkirk finish equal on goal difference on Sunday, Hibs will be awarded second place as they have the better head-to-head record in this season's fixtures between the two clubs.

Darren McGregor, John McGinn and Jason Cummings have all been named in the Scottish Championship Team of the Year so the awards keep coming for Hibs players. McGregor's choice is particularly pleasing and hopefully it will boost his confidence going into the crucial closing stages of the season.

The war of words between Peter Houston and Alan Stubbs rumbles on. Stubbs has suggested that the pressure going into this weekend's final fixtures is on Falkirk. Houston has said that he is feeling so little pressure that he shot three birdies during a round of golf at St Andrews this week. He also less than elegantly described suggestions that Falkirk might crumble as 'crap'.

James Keatings, who has been awarded a hat-trick against Dumbarton after being credited with the third goal which had initially looked like an own goal, is going for his third successive promotion from the Championship, having achieved it in the last two seasons with Hamilton and Hearts. Interestingly, when Hamilton were going for goals to boost their goal difference on the last day of season 2013–14, they managed to win 10–2 but still couldn't stop Dundee achieving automatic promotion. Hibs would certainly take that score line on Sunday against Queen of the South.

Decision Day in the Championship is imminent and after it we will know whether Hibs have finished second or third in the league for season 2015–16. At the moment, Falkirk with their three-goal advantage in goal difference, are very much in the driving seat. In truth, Hibs should have wrapped up second spot some time ago. Surrendering two goals in four minutes to Falkirk at home was really the nadir of their season although losing at Alloa three days earlier wasn't far behind it. Peter Houston, as ever, is talking the talk, let's hope that when Queen of the South come to Easter Road, Hibs can walk the walk.

1–13 May 2016

Play-Off Despair

Speculation about Stubbs future – play-off win over Raith – injury time sickener at Falkirk

Hibs have beaten Queen of the South 2–0 but because Falkirk beat Morton 1–0 at home, it wasn't enough to gain Hibs second place so they now face the possibility of playing seven vital matches in twenty days at the end of a gruelling season. Falkirk secured second spot by a margin of two goals.

Queen of the South, to quote their caretaker manager Gavin Skelton, were 'determined not to get turned over'. They defended in depth and displayed huge work rate and concentration. Hibs, as has been the case throughout Alan Stubbs' reign, could have and should have scored more goals. James Keatings and Liam Henderson both spurned clear goal-scoring opportunities, there were several other near things and James Atkinson in the Queens' goal, like so many other goalkeepers who come to Easter Road, had an inspired ninety minutes. Niklas Gunnarsson and

Jason Cummings (off the bench) scored Hibs goals and Mark Millar of Queen of the South was shown a straight red card for a nasty, cynical lunge to scythe down John McGinn when he was in full flight.

Falkirk, meanwhile, were awarded a dubious penalty which they missed and saw Morton have a goal chalked off late in the match. Peter Houston described his players as having demonstrated, 'attitude, commitment and desire,' all season. He was right. They have enjoyed their fair share of luck as well.

Hibs now travel to Scotland's form team Raith Rovers in midweek for the first leg of the play-off quarter-final. Alan Stubbs said after the Queens game that Hibs now potentially face seven cup finals. He is completely correct in his assessment. Raith will be ready for them and really up for this match. Nothing but Hibs' best and bravest will be good enough.

Stubbs refuted suggestions during his press conference that finishing third in the Championship is failure for Hibs. He is right in as much as overall the season has been a success but Hibs should have been capable of finishing higher than Falkirk. Some critics are cruelly suggesting that Hibs have finished third in a two-horse race. That is unfair. Falkirk have been a team of substance all season. They have only lost four league matches and, time and time again, they have scored very late goals to win vital points.

Where Hibs did fall down was in losing nine points in total to Dumbarton and Alloa and in also losing to Morton, Queen of the South and Raith Rovers. They shouldn't have conceded a two-goal lead against a ten-man Falkirk team in the last four minutes at Easter Road either. Just one more point from any of these fixtures or even two more chances converted from the many that were squandered in the course of the season would have seen Hibs finish second rather than third.

John McGinn has recently described Jason Cummings as 'a brilliant boy'. Cummings has just come out and claimed that Raith and Falkirk will be scared of Hibs in the play-offs. I don't think that that comment is brilliant. I consider it to be ill-advised, as it will clearly fire up both Raith and Falkirk.

Ivan Sproule has retired from football at the age of thirty-five. During his first spell at Easter Road, Sproule was an exciting, tricky winger with electric pace who was capable of both scoring and creating goals. No Hibs fan will ever forget his match-winning hat-trick against Rangers at Ibrox during the Tony Mowbray era. It would be nice to think that Jason Cummings could make himself a truly 'brilliant boy' by scoring three of the best against the Ibrox men when this year's Scottish Cup Final comes round on 21 May.

The first of what could potentially be several 'D Days' for Hibs beckons. They travel to Stark's Park, Kirkcaldy, to face Ray McKinnon's Raith Rovers. McKinnon has been talking up his team's chances and doing his best to put all the pressure on Hibs. Predictably, he has referred to Jason Cumming's remarks and made it clear that his team will do their talking on the park. I really like Jason but sometimes he speaks without considering the consequences and creates problems for himself and the team. Raith are big and powerful and bursting with energy and motivation and on their own less-than-perfect home surface will be quite a handful for Hibs.

Dylan McGeouch played for twenty minutes against Queen of the South on Sunday and in that short space of time looked like the class act that he undoubtedly is. Today he announced that he hopes that he won't break down again before the end of the season but cautioned the fans not to expect him to play ninety minutes just yet.

Hibs have lost 1–0 to Raith Rovers in the play-off quarter-final first leg. Raith scored in the seventy-fifth minute from a header from a corner. The scorer, Harry Panayiotou, the substitute, was completely unmarked. Hibs had fifteen attempts on goal in the match while Raith had three. Failure to convert chances and lack of concentration in defence, two recurring factors throughout Alan Stubbs' reign, have caused Hibs problems again. This time the problems are major because if Hibs don't overturn this deficit on Saturday, they are condemned to another season of Championship football, which is not an attractive proposition. After the game, Alan Stubbs criticised the pitch and the officials. He never ever attaches blame to his players. Certainly not in public anyway. Maybe that is the right way for a manager to go about things.

My daughter and I have queued for almost nine hours for tickets for the Scottish Cup final. To service a queue that stretched along the interior of the West Stand and beyond that on to the track at the side of the pitch, Hibs had five ticket windows open. Some people were renewing season tickets as well as purchasing cup final tickets. Leeann Dempster has apologised. Clearly the club's current systems cannot cope with major demand. The banter in the queue was great, though. There was a mixture of optimism and fatalism. Some people think that this is Hibs' time. Others are resigned to more disappointment but intend to be at Hampden just in case things do in fact go well. Publicly I am being cautious, but inside I have a growing feeling that this just might be Hibs' year.

Ray McKinnon, the Raith Rovers manager, who is being hotly tipped to replace Mixu Paatelainen as manager of Dundee

United – the club he played for with distinction of course – is piling the pressure on Hibs ahead of Saturday's play-off quarter-final second leg. Stressing how much this game means to Hibs and how devastating it will be for them if they lose it, McKinnon stated that he expects Hibs to be full of nerves.

Two things are for sure. Dylan McGeouch must play from the start whether he is reluctant to do so or not and the Hibs support has to turn out in numbers, get behind the team and stay behind it. The fans' backing will be a vital part of this hugely crucial encounter.

In the cup final ticket queue at Easter Road, one Hibee wailed, 'I love this team, I love this club, I love the green and white strips and I have supported them all my life but why do they always let me down?' Hopefully they will not let him down over the coming days or weeks.

Alan Stubbs has told the fans that they have a big role to play in the second leg against Raith. Responding to Ray McKinnon's suggestion that the crowd might get restless and start to criticise the team if things don't go well from the start, Stubbs has asked the Hibs support to 'show what brilliant fans they are'. I think those of us who follow Hibs have put up with a great deal of disappointment but we always come back for more. We deserve a good performance, which includes ruthless finishing and proper defending. If we get that, we should be capable of going through. Stubbs says Easter Road has to be 'jumping but patient'. I think that puts it perfectly.

Hibs started the Raith Rovers game brilliantly. John McGinn and Darren McGregor scored within twelve minutes and Easter Road was rocking. For the remainder of the match, Hibs created more and better chances but Raith with their huge physical presence and total commitment always stayed in the game. Raith forced a ninety-fourth-minute corner and all Hibs fans could be forgiven for thinking 'Here we go again' but Conrad Logan made a great catch when the ball came over and the tie was won.

Now Hibs move on to face Falkirk twice in the next six days and with such a short turnaround, tiredness must be a factor for Hibs who have played fifty-one games this season to Falkirk's thirty-eight but adrenalin and desire can take a team a long way.

There has been an unwelcome distraction in recent days because Bolton Wanderers are apparently considering making Alan Stubbs their new manager. Stubbs played for Bolton for six years of course and it is in Lancashire where his family have remained during his two-year stint with Hibs. He may very well be tempted to go. For the moment, though, he is making it clear that he is fully focused on Hibs.

Mickey Weir writing in his *Evening News* column thinks Hibs will beat Falkirk. I hope he is right. Mickey bases his prediction on a feeling that Hibs' 'big game players' (presumably he means John McGinn, Anthony Stokes, Jason Cummings and Dylan McGeouch) will rise to the occasion. Again, I hope he is right.

There was an interesting article on Pat Fenlon in the *Scotsman*. Fenlon is now managing Shamrock Rovers back in Ireland but inevitably he was asked about the 5–1 Scottish Cup final defeat to Hearts. He was specifically asked if he regretted making the rude 'Get it right up you' gesture to the Hearts support as they goaded him towards the end of that most painful of games. The gesture landed him in trouble with the SFA. His answer was direct. He said that not only did he not regret making his gesture. It was, in fact, the only part of the day which he had enjoyed.

Almost before they had a chance to draw breath after the two matches against Raith Rovers, Hibs have played the first leg of the play-off semi-final against Falkirk at Easter Road and what a game it was. Since dropping into the Championship, Hibs have played Falkirk nine times. In one match at the end of last season, Hibs won comfortably to secure second place in the league. Earlier this season, Hibs won 1–0 at Falkirk with a disputed penalty. The other seven have all followed a similar pattern. Hibs dominate the game, Falkirk soak up pressure, score on the break and come away with a win or a draw, which they don't deserve. The latest meeting continued that trend.

Hibs controlled the first half without looking particularly penetrative but Falkirk scored a fortunate deflected goal to go in one up at half time. After the break Hibs blew Falkirk away. Liam Henderson and Darren McGregor scored. McGregor should have scored another and Anthony Stokes missed a great chance. David McCracken handled the ball in the box. It was indisputably clear and a definite penalty. Referee Alan Muir who had given Hibs the contentious penalty at Falkirk earlier in the season was clearly determined not to award them another one whether it was contentious or not and he turned his back on all claims. After the match, media opinion was unanimous that it was a major refereeing error and should have been a penalty.

Ten minutes from the end, Falkirk's Bob McHugh, who specialises in late goals, shot straight at Conrad Logan. The Polar Bear who had been so impressive since coming into Hibs team made a complete mess of things and allowed the ball to squirm out of his hands and into the net for a most undeserved equaliser.

Post-match, Alan Stubbs was incandescent about the referee's failure to give such a blatant penalty. It can't be changed though and Falkirk have got away with it again. It is now all down to a winner takes all shoot out at Falkirk on Friday night.

When they meet Falkirk in the play-off semi-final second leg at the Falkirk Stadium, Hibs will be playing their fifth match in just thirteen days. It is a big ask and the players' physical fitness and mental strength will be put to the test. Both Dylan McGeouch and Darren McGregor have been talking positively about the game, which is good to hear. McGeouch's return from injury has been a real positive. He is a superb player and, when he is fit and available, he makes a great difference to Hibs.

Blackburn Rovers have joined Bolton Wanderers in being interested in making Alan Stubbs their new manager. Stubbs is resolutely refusing to discuss such speculation and continues to insist that he is solely focused on helping Hibs win promotion and lift the Scottish Cup. He seems very genuine in this aim when you listen to him speaking.

Meanwhile, recently relegated Dundee United have wasted no time in installing Ray McKinnon as their new manager. If he does as well at Tannadice as he did at Stark's Park, United will be a force to be reckoned with in the Championship next season.

Hibs have lost 3–2 to Falkirk and will spend a third consecutive season in the Scottish Championship. Alan Stubbs left Jason Cummings on the bench and started the game with

James Keatings partnering Anthony Stokes up front. Falkirk had the better of the early stages and went ahead through Blair Alston.

Hibs fought back into the game and Keatings scored twice to give them the half-time lead. His first came from the penalty spot and David McCracken, who brought him down, should have been sent off. Referee Craig Thomson did not even produce the yellow card.

Hibs could have added to their lead in the second half and, with eleven minutes left, seemed comfortable. Then a misdirected headed clearance from David Gray fell at the feet of Luke Leahy twenty-five yards from goal and he rifled a rocket shot low past Conrad Logan. Jason Cummings came on and rattled the crossbar from thirty-five yards. Anthony Stokes then missed a great-headed chance in stoppage time before Falkirk won a throw in in the ninety-second minute. What followed was as inevitable as it was avoidable. In came a long throw. Hibs didn't deal with it convincingly. The ball ran loose to Bob McHugh and the scourge of Hibs whenever these two teams meet buried a sweet volley in the corner of Hibs net. Once again, Hibs had outplayed Falkirk and once again they had failed to beat them. This time, though, the final outcome was not a draw but the costliest and cruellest of defeats.

Forty-eight hours have passed since Hibs' late, late defeat to Falkirk. I am still hurting badly and still trying to work out how Hibs can dominate two games against Falkirk and end up losing on aggregate. Over the two games, the referees were kind to Falkirk but that is where the excuses stop. Hibs can't blame anyone but themselves for missed chances, goalkeeping errors and defensive frailty. A year ago, Peter Houston stated that Hibs couldn't defend balls into their box. He was right and twelve months down the line we still don't deal consistently with corners, crosses and long throws. The worst part of it, though, is that Hibs are a better team than Falkirk. When we meet them, we usually outplay them. It is just that our superiority is rarely displayed in the scoreline. Falkirk's capacity to score late goals is remarkable.

14–20 May 2016

Cup Final Countdown

Reflecting on failure to win promotion – looking ahead to Hampden

Alan Stubbs is being equivocal about his future and it is possible that he intends to leave Hibs at the end of the season. Has he been a success? Well, Hibs are more attractive to watch and he has brought in some good players but – and it's a big but – we continually lose games we should win and we are stuck in the second tier of Scottish football for a record third season. Stubbs' reign will ultimately be defined by what happens in next Saturday's Scottish Cup final against Rangers. If Hibs lose, he will be regarded as a 'nearly man'. If they win, he will become immortal. Although I am still not admitting it publicly because I don't want to tempt fate, I genuinely have an inkling that next Saturday at Hampden could be a significant one in Hibs' history. Irrespective of the result of the Scottish Cup final, I would like Alan Stubbs to be at Easter Road next season.

Hibs have let their wonderful fans down far too often. It is payback time, and Stubbs and his players really need to repay the Hibs support for their unwavering loyalty over many difficult seasons. Another dismal capitulation or wasted opportunity at Hampden doesn't bear thinking about.

Marvin Bartley has today issued an apology to the Hibs supporters and to his manager Alan Stubbs. Bartley admitted that by losing to Falkirk and squandering the chance to win promotion he and his fellow players had failed.

He cited the reasons for this failure as being an inability to convert chances and weak defending at crucial times. This is a refrain that has echoed through this journal. Two examples from the final moments of the second-leg play-off disaster sum things up. First, Anthony Stokes missed a close-range free header. Not only did his effort lack conviction, he made contact with his shoulder rather than his head. Then when Falkirk's long throw came into the Hibs penalty area in the ninety-second minute, not for the first time no one dealt with it decisively and Fraser Fyvie who was closest to the goal scorer Bob McHugh reacted too slowly in contrast to McHugh who attacked the ball with intent.

Marvin Bartley posed a question about 'lack of desire' on Hibs' part. It is a valid question. They seem to wait for things to happen and hope that everything turns out all right. Falkirk and other teams make things happen. I don't think that Hibs lack desire to win. They just seem to be found wanting at crucial times in games. I am not at all sure why that should be the case. I am certain though that there will be no lack of desire at Hampden on Saturday.

Be in no doubt though that the players were suffering. Darren McGregor ('one of our own') said this: 'We all understood what was on the line against Falkirk so we are hurting. We'd worked so hard and to lose it in the manner that we did was devastating. We had three hours to win and we felt that we had done enough to win but we didn't. Falkirk came up with the goods and we have had to resign ourselves to another year in the Championship. The Scottish Cup final is a great opportunity for us to end the season on a massive high. I'm sure a lot of Hibs fans would see that as going a long way towards redemption.' That was exactly the kind of fighting talk that the supporters wanted to hear.

Liam Henderson also reflected on the Falkirk defeat. He said, 'I don't think we deserved to go out but that's football and that's why people pay to come and watch it. It can be a magical game at times but at other times it can be a terrible game.' Wise words from a young man. Hibs fans had experienced the 'terrible' side of things at Falkirk. Maybe they would experience the 'magical' side at Hampden.

Henderson finished by saying, 'The Cup final is game fifty-four of the season for us, the last one, and we have to throw everything we've got at it.' The fans couldn't ask for any more than that.

Commenting in his column in the *Evening News* on the possibility of a mass exodus of players from Easter Road in the summer, Mickey Weir acknowledged that a lot of the Hibs squad are highly rated and in demand. He then pondered why, if these players are so good, they had failed to get the club promoted, which seems a very fair question. It's not about promotion now, though. It's about Scottish Cup glory.

Understandably, Alan Stubbs has kept a low profile this week but he resurfaced at Hampden today to carry out his round of pre-Scottish Cup final interviews. He claimed that his players had fully got over last Friday's final-minute capitulation at

Falkirk. I wish that I could say the same for myself. I am still hurting badly. Our club desperately needed promotion.

Stubbs says that he has told the Hibs squad to give every last drop of energy for the cause on Saturday. He wants them to be so tired that they will 'crawl off the pitch' at the end of the match. They are certainly going to need to expend every ounce of effort to compete with Rangers' passing game.

Stubbs also said that with the exception of Farid El Alagui, Hibs have a fully fit squad. Presumably that statement includes Dylan McGeouch, who again went off with groin problems during the first half at Falkirk.

Fitness is relative with McGeouch. This season he has rarely been fit enough to start games and when he has played from the start he has hardly ever managed to last the course. A fit and firing McGeouch is huge for Hibs. He is a highly talented player and it would be a massive boost if he could manage ninety minutes on Saturday.

Alan Stubbs also admitted that although he couldn't say so publicly, it was always going to be a big ask for Hibs to win their way through three play-off double headers and lift the Scottish Cup as well. He contended that defeat to Falkirk has given his players more recovery time and that will help their quest for the Scottish. Of course, if we had finished second rather than third, we wouldn't have faced the prospect of three play-off double headers.

That's all in the past now though. What is done is done. At last, I have managed to move from post-play-off despondency to pre-Scottish Cup final excitement and anticipation.

21–31 May 2016

Scottish Cup Glory

Pre-match build up – the Holy Grail attained – pitch invasion – the Victory Parade – farewell to Stubbs

Today I will travel to Hampden with my wife, four children and three of my grandchildren. We will travel in the hope that Hibs will beat Rangers and lift the Scottish Cup for the first time since 1902. Robert Burns died 106 years before Hibs' last win in the Scottish. The longer period of 114 years has passed since that distant triumph. That says it all.

In 1902, Real Madrid were formed and Newton Heath changed its name to Manchester United. That is how long it is since Hibs have won the Scottish Cup. In that same year, 'Land of Hope and Glory' was composed. Hibs fans are certainly hoping for glory at Hampden. Ten losing finals have passed since we beat Celtic 1–0 through Andy McGeachan's goal all these years ago and I have been present at quite a few of them. This day may be a date with destiny and long overdue history may be made. It has to happen some time, doesn't it?

Hibernian Football Club, the team I have loved all my life, have won the 2015–16 Scottish Cup. I can barely believe that I have just typed that sentence. After a lifetime of attending losing Scottish Cup semi-finals and finals, I had resigned myself to the fact that, like so many other dedicated Hibees before me, I would not live to see the Hibs lift the Scottish Cup. Well, that has all changed now and what a weekend it has been!

We travelled through on a supporters' bus and the mood was surprisingly upbeat and optimistic. There was a general consensus among the fans that this just might be Hibs' day and that was before any drink had been consumed.

My son Dominic usually has a good instinct for how games might turn out. He feels it in his bones whether Hibs will win or lose and, more often than not, he is correct. He announced that he was sure that Hibs were going to win. That was a good sign. He was so sure in fact that he had placed two bets. His first wager was on Hibs to win the Scottish Cup. The second was for Anthony Stokes to score.

The bus convener had booked a private room in a pub near Hampden for our group and by 12.15pm, there was a long queue at the bar. As the alcohol kicked in and the volume of singing continued to rise, some of the assembled company even indulged in some dancing to accompany their vocals. All generations of Hibees were present and were united in their desire to see their beloved team make history. The full Hibs repertoire was worked through but one song received multiple airings. The chorus of 'When the Hibs go up to lift the Scottish Cup, we'll be there' was sung again and again. It was to prove a prophetic line.

One fan in his twenties was dressed in a Superman costume. Another, of more mature vintage who was clad totally in green and was sporting a magnificent set of dreadlocks, asked him somewhat brusquely what his choice of apparel had to do with Hibs. The younger supporter pointed to the logo on his chest which read 'Super John McGinn' and that was that question very decisively answered.

Superman's friend was dressed from head to toe in green lycra. His outfit was of the all-in-one variety. He announced that he was going to the toilet. Superman responded, 'See you in two hours'.

Going up to the ground, I met quite a few people I knew and they were all of the opinion that it was time for Hibs' Hampden hoodoo to be banished once and for all. Alan Stubbs had decided that a 3-5-2 formation, which had served him well against Rangers in the past, was the best way to achieve this. There were two changes in personnel from the Falkirk game. Liam Fontaine came into central defence and Jason Cummings partnered Anthony Stokes up front. Liam Henderson and James Keatings unluckily dropped to the bench and Dylan McGeouch was fit to start, which was great news.

We took our seats in the South Stand very close to where we had sat in 2007 when Hibs had defeated Kilmarnock 5–1 to win the League Cup. Would this prove to be a good omen? We looked over to the North Stand, where our fellow Hibs supporters were holding up a banner that simply said, 'Time for Heroes'.

Within three minutes of kick-off, Stokes had provided real hope that this might indeed be Hibs day. Picking up a pass from Jason

Cummings, he cut in from the left and placed a superbly precise shot into the far corner of the net leaving Wes Foderingham helpless in the Rangers goal.

Hibs continued to play well and create chances but, in virtually their first meaningful attack, Rangers equalised when Kenny Miller rose above Darren McGregor and bulleted an unstoppable header past Conrad Logan. Within minutes Stokes, who was having by far his best game since returning to Easter Road, made space for himself and fired in a great shot from twenty-five yards. Unfortunately, the ball hit the inside of the post and bounced to safety. Was Hibs Hampden curse about to strike again?

Then Rangers suffered some similar misfortune as Miller rose unmarked to head against the bar. Hibs' marking was conspicuous by its absence but for once they survived such an incident.

My half-time thoughts were optimistic. I was calm and my positive premonition hadn't wavered.

The second half was evenly contested until Rangers again scored from nowhere and what a goal it was. Andy Halliday picked the ball up on Rangers' left, moved forward without challenge and rocketed a howitzer of a left-foot shot past Logan. The big goalkeeper expressed his dissatisfaction at the weakness of the defending in no uncertain terms. In the past, Hibs' heads would have gone down at this point and the game would have been over. Alan Stubbs' team was made of sterner stuff though.

With ten minutes to go, Liam Henderson sent over a tempting corner and there was the outstanding Stokes waiting at the near post to head Hibs level. At this point, even I, who had suffered so many previous disappointments, began to feel that destiny might just be on the horizon and so it proved.

In the ninety-second minute, Anthony Stokes drove into the Rangers' penalty area yet again. As he pulled his foot back, I heard myself shouting, 'Go on Stokesy. This for history.' Stokes fired the ball across goal but Foderingham diverted it away from the waiting James Keatings who had come on for Jason Cummings and out for a corner. History was only to be delayed though. It wasn't to be denied.

Liam Henderson again took the corner and, as the ball hung in the air, captain David Gray timed his run and leap perfectly and bulleted home the most magnificent header imaginable. Cue mass hysteria in the Hibs end. One newspaper report later summed up the captain's goal perfectly. It said, 'Gray appeared to want to win that header more than anyone ever wanted to win a header in their lives.' That historic header instantaneously earned David Gray the eternal gratitude and unending affection of the Hibs support.

The next two minutes felt like two hours before eventually referee Steven McLean blew for full time and 114 years of hurt had finally been brought to an end. No longer could the annual ritual in the media and among Hearts fans of baiting Hibs when the Scottish Cup came round be indulged in. How long was it since Hibs had won the Scottish Cup? Eh, actually it was a mere thirty seconds!

There was unfettered joy among the Hibs support. Scarves were raised, flags were waved and songs were sung. Minds turned to friends and family no longer with us who would be sharing this moment from the heights of heaven (the angels up above). In our case, we thought of Margaret's late dad Arthur, who had passed on his love of Hibernian to his sons and daughters, and her brothers Michael and Terry, both taken from us tragically young in recent years. They were all Hibs men through and through and should have been with us to share this triumph. I have no doubt that they would have been leading the celestial Hibs supporters' club in a rousing version of 'Glory Glory to the Hibees'.

Then there was a pitch invasion. Hibs fans full of exuberance, exultation and relief began to run on to the playing surface. Some lifted turf while others swung on the cross bar which eventually gave way. Most were intent purely on celebration.

The scenes were reminiscent of those at Wembley in 1967 when the Jim Baxter-inspired Scots beat Alf Ramsey's World Cup winners 3–2 and again in 1977 when Scotland once more triumphed in London. Things changed when a small number of Hibs and Rangers supporters came together inside the Rangers' half. The police broke things up quickly, and soon mounted and foot-patrol police were ringing the Hibs' half of the pitch. The vast majority of the Hibs support stayed in the stands and called for those on the field to return to their seats, which they eventually did. When order was restored, it was time for the cup to be presented and this time it wasn't going to Hearts, Rangers or Celtic or even Airdrie, Aberdeen or Clyde who had all beaten Hibs in previous finals, it was going to be Hibernian Football Club after 114 interminable years of waiting and longing.

It was an unforgettable moment when David Gray and his teammates went up to lift the Scottish Cup and receive their medals. Grown men and women cried tears of happiness and told themselves that, yes, it really had happened at last!

As David Gray held up world football's oldest trophy, it occurred to me that the right back in the 1902 team was also a Gray. His name was Archie and he would have been very proud of his 2016 namesake. It also dawned on me that despite the opprobrium poured on Hibs' performances in the Scottish Cup down all the decades, only five teams have lifted the trophy more times than Hibs. They are Celtic and Rangers, of course, Hearts, Aberdeen and Queen's Park, who won it ten times in the competition's early days.

Standing at David Gray's side as he lifted the 'Scottish' were Lewis Stevenson and Paul Hanlon. Two great servants to Hibs, Lewis and Paul had both suffered the heartbreak of the 2012 and 2013 Scottish Cup finals. Now it was their turn to celebrate.

Sadly the team's lap of honour was cancelled for safety reasons, so those who had spilled on to the pitch had deprived the support and the players of the chance to celebrate together in the traditional style.

That was not going to be allowed to detract from an amazing victory though. After the presentation of the cup, the players, still on the rostrum, joined the fans in belting out a heartfelt and emotional version of 'Sunshine on Leith'. There then followed a full rendition of 'Glory Glory to the Hibees', which was sung with the greatest gusto. The line 'I only want to say the Scottish Cup is in the bag' was delivered with unbridled passion and delight.

The crowd took a long time to disperse as celebrations moved from inside the stands to the concourses below where delirious Hibees greeted friends and family and all the time the singing continued. Walking out of Hampden as Scottish Cup winners at last was an indescribably good feeling. We hadn't managed to get a programme before the match but the authorities, with commendable commercial acumen, had put the match-day magazines back on sale as the crowds made their way out of the stadium. The lady who was selling them near us was in danger of being bowled over as fans clamoured to acquire a souvenir of this most special of days. She muttered, in her strong Glaswegian accent, 'For God's sake, I've sold ten times mair programmes efter the game than I did before it.'

We returned to the bus to learn that our convener had negotiated with the bus driver to delay his departure. This created time for celebrations of a more liquid variety. What a feeling it was to buy my family their first drink after Hibs first Scottish Cup win in 114 years.

As our bus entered Princes Street on the way home, a spectacular rainbow illuminated Edinburgh Castle. It felt like a sign from above.

Back in the house, Margaret and I had something to eat and a couple more drinks. We then watched the highlights of the final on *Sportscene* before retiring for the night emotionally drained and in a state of exhausted euphoria. The rest of the family couldn't get into any of the pubs in Easter Road as they were all full to capacity so they adjourned to a hostelry close to home to continue their revels.

In the meantime, the team had returned to Easter Road to show off the cup to those who were gathered at the stadium before beginning their evening's festivities in one of the function suites.

Throughout Leith, the pubs were bouncing with uncontained joy. It was Hogmanay in May and the song 'the Hibs are having a party, the Hearts are in their bed' received many an airing.

Alan Stubbs and his players are now Hibernian History Men

and they deserve the highest praise and commendation. That is exactly what they got next day when they paraded the Scottish Cup in a golden open top bus from the City Chambers down Leith Walk to Leith Links. Crowds of more than 150,000 turned out to cheer them and when the bus came to a halt at the spot at the Links where we were, the happiest of celebrations took place.

The fans serenaded the team, the players reciprocated by serenading the fans and some songs were roared out in unison. The Scottish Cup was raised on high over and over again. Even club owner Sir Tom Farmer took a bow from the top deck of the bus and was rewarded with a rendition of 'There's only one Tom Farmer'.

Pat Stanton was at the Links too. Commenting on the fact that the open-top bus was delayed in reaching the Links due to the size of the crowds, Pat said, 'When you've waited 114 years, what's another couple of hours?'

A large group of younger fans had taken over one of the mounds on the links and even after the team had entered their coach and left the scene, they carried on singing and bouncing with jubilation for quite some time. A small corner of Leith Links had forever become Hibernian Hill.

At the Links, we met lots of people we knew, and hugs and handshakes were the order of the day. Everyone said the same thing which was, 'I never thought that I would live to see this day.' Well, live to see it we did. One person said to me, 'Your smile is so wide and so fixed that if I forcefed you six bitter lemons, it still wouldn't go away.' That sums up how I felt.

In truth a lot of Hibs supporters felt exactly the same. Here are some of their comments.

'I watched the game on TV. At seventy-seven years old, my nerves can't take going to Hampden any more. At full time I was shaking. I never thought that I would see today. Now I can die happy.'

'It's unbelievable. My dad waited his whole life to see this but he passed away three years ago. My sister and I are sobbing with emotion.'

'My granddad's granddad never saw Hibs winning the Scottish Cup. 114 years and I am the one who gets to witness it at the age of twenty-two. I don't think that there's been a happier day in my life.'

'I knew that today would end in tears. I am just so glad that they were tears of joy.'

'After 114 years, we've finally done it. It's won. Thank God. The bairn was crying with twenty minutes to go because she thought that we were beat. I was crying with her at the end because we'd won.'

'I'm seventy-four and have been a Hibs fan since the early fifties. Loads of times I've gone to Hampden thinking we would win the Scottish Cup and we've gone down. If the big man gives me the nod now at least I have seen Hibs win the Scottish Cup.'

'The fans going on the pitch was an emotional thing. When you wait 100-odd years for something to happen, the emotions take over.'

Alan Stubbs has responded very modestly to attaining immortal status. He has given all the credit to his players and will auction his winner's medal for charity. Jason Cummings has said that the feeling of winning the Scottish couldn't possibly be topped so he might as well retire now. I am sure that he won't.

Lewis Stevenson who has served Hibs so faithfully for so long gave an emotional interview to Hibs TV in which he admitted that, like the fans, he had started to think that the Holy Grail would never be won.

In another interview, Lewis revealed that he is going to get his first tattoo. He said, 'The tattoo will feature the date of the final and a picture of the cup and it will say "We Hibsed it!". Lewis, with typical honesty added, 'We know the pain we have put the Hibs fans through. I've felt it. I thought at one point today, we were destined for failure again. Thank God we weren't.' Well said, that man. Lewis is the only player in Hibs history to win both a Scottish Cup and a League Cup winners' medal with the club.

Anthony Stokes, who was simply magnificent throughout the game, said, 'I am just thankful to be part of the squad which has managed to do it.' Well Stokesy, Hibs fans were very thankful for your two goals and for the way you played.

John McGinn who rediscovered his outstanding early-season form at the business end of the campaign had this to say: 'It's crazy to think that we will all be Hibs legends now. I've been told that I will never need to buy another drink in Edinburgh so I will be going out every week! Obviously it took a few days to get the play-off defeat out of our system. We failed to get promotion and it made us all the more determined to win the Scottish Cup and bring the trophy back to Leith. At 2–1 down, I still believed that we could win it. Ever since the Hearts game at Tynecastle earlier in the competition, we've known that we can come back to win.' McGinn finished by cheekily suggesting that Hibs were now targeting the Europa League.

Alan Mackie, who is the School Support Officer at St John's Primary School where I used to be headteacher, told me that he had been speaking to Leigh Griffiths who had shared this story with him. Leigh said to Alan that, as John McGinn was climbing the stairs to the rostrum to be presented with his Scottish Cup Winner's medal, he leaned over from where he was sitting to congratulate John and tell him that he would swap anything he had achieved in football to be standing in McGinn's shoes right at that moment. That tells just how much of a true Hibee Leigh is.

Darren McGregor, with his tongue firmly in his cheek, said that he would use his win bonus to take his partner Erin to Gullane on holiday instead of going to Portobello as he had originally planned! I am sure that Darren will be heading for rather more exotic climes.

David Gray said that he and Liam Fontaine had discussed the possibility of a stoppage-time winner in their hotel room on the eve of the final. Now exactly what they had dared to dream of had come to pass. Gray dedicated the victory to 106-year-old Hibs fan Sam Martinez, who had waited longer than anyone for the magic moment to arrive.

An emotional Liam Henderson spoke about his imminent return to Celtic but summed up his feelings in these words: 'Hibs fans are unreal and I don't feel that I have been on loan here. I am just very thankful that I could repay the fans and sign out on a high at the end. Hibs will be a part of me in the years to come.' These were lovely words from 'Hendo', whose pinpoint corner kicks played such a big part in Hibs' triumph.

The great Pat Stanton said that he had sat with his grandson Quinn at Hampden only a few yards away from where he sat with his dad at the 1958 final against Clyde. Pat would have been just thirteen years old then.

Former club captain Jackie McNamara was also in an emotional state. Jackie commented, 'That was why Anthony Stokes was brought to the club. I never thought that I would see the day when Hibs lifted the Scottish Cup. I reckon that I will be crying about this for a long time.'

Movie star and lifelong Hibee Dougray Scott posted a photo of the Hibs fans celebrating on the pitch online. He said, 'This is what 114 years of hurt looks like. Relieved! I love this club. I'm crying!'

Andy Murray's mum Judy tweeted a picture of the fans on the pitch and quoted the Proclaimers' lyrics, 'On our way from misery to happiness today'. She added, 'Glory, Glory to the Hibees'.

Unsurprisingly, the Scottish press and media, particularly those sections of it which have most of their readership in the West of Scotland, have made much of the post-match pitch invasion.

The best starting point when attempting to evaluate how serious the pitch invasion was is to look at exactly what happened. When the referee blew the final whistle, a spontaneous outpouring of joy and relief led to Hibs supporters running on to the pitch to celebrate. Carried away with the understandable emotion of the moment, others quickly followed them. I would estimate that around 5,000 fans came onto the pitch. That means that 16,000 stayed in the stands. The vast majority of those who were on the pitch cavorted about waving their scarves and hugging each other. They were jubilant not malicious. A small number let themselves and the club down. They moved towards the Rangers end and there was a coming together between Hibs and Rangers supporters. This was regrettable, as were the alleged attacks on Rangers players. These scenes were quickly contained though and euphoria was once again the order of the day. As the fans in the stands began to shout 'Off, off, off', the revellers started to move back to their seats and eventually the pitch was cleared.

When you watch BBC Scotland's post-match footage and look at the Hibees who are coming on to the field and look at the crowd as they acclaim David Gray lifting the Scottish Cup, you see reasonable, respectable people who are glowing with happiness. These are not people who are bent on causing trouble.

Yet Hibs have been pilloried in the press, on the radio and on television in the most extreme terms. Some of the language used by pundits and pressmen has, in my opinion, been way over the top. The SFA Chief Executive Stewart Regan wasted no time in saying post-match that the final would be remembered for the scenes that followed it rather than for the match itself or the outcome of the match. Try telling any Hibs fan that.

Rangers Football Club have issued two statements. The first was produced with indecent haste shortly after the cup final finished. They have criticised a wide range of parties, including Nicola Sturgeon the First Minister because she had had the temerity to congratulate Hibs on their victory. Incidentally, Labour MSP Ian Gray tabled a parliamentary motion congratulating Hibs on their win. Rangers were noticeably slow though to take responsibility for the actions of their own followers.

Jason Cummings, never the most diplomatic of men, gave his verdict on the match's aftermath. Jason said, 'It's passion. It's football. Everyone knows what a day it is for Hibs, a historical day, the first time in 114 years. I don't think the club will be punished. You've scored a last-minute winner in the Scottish Cup, a competition you've not won for 114 years. I wouldn't be sitting on my chair. I'd be on the pitch. That's what you do.'

Paul Hanlon expressed a similar point of view. Paul said, 'You can't blame the fans. They have had enough suffering over the years. You can't blame them for going mad. It's no more than they deserve.'

Sections of the press and media very much want Hibs to be punished though. There have been calls for, among other things, Hibs to be banned from Europe, Hibs to be excluded from next season's Scottish Cup or Hibs to be hit with a record fine. These suggestions in my opinion are ludicrous and smack of vindictiveness.

Hibs have issued statements expressing regret at what happened, giving an assurance that they will fully co-operate with any enquiries and making it clear that they will take strong actions against any Hibs supporters who have broken the law or behaved inappropriately. At the time of going to press, life bans and indefinite bans have already been issued to fans who transgressed at Hampden. What more are Hibs supposed to do? They were not responsible for crowd control at the cup final. That responsibility lay with the SFA, Police Scotland and the stewards who were on duty. Yet Rod Petrie has been the subject of unwarranted criticism.

The Hibs supporters should have stayed in the stands. Damaging the goalposts and ripping up pieces of turf weren't the best judged of actions. Mind you, when Scotland fans did exactly the same things at Wembley in the 1960s and 70s, it was reported as mass celebration for famous victories.

If any Hibs (or Rangers) fan is found guilty of assault, then they should be given the punishment they undoubtedly deserve.

Both the SFA and Police Scotland have launched enquiries. The findings of these enquiries will be awaited with interest. Let us hope that a sense of perspective will be retained.

The *Edinburgh Evening News* summed up the post-match happenings perfectly in its Leader Column after the cup final when it said, 'It is a terrible shame that this wonderful time for everyone associated with the club has been adversely affected by the bad behaviour of a small minority ... the vast majority of Hibs fans who behaved impeccably should not suffer for the idiocy of the few. It is a shame that they did not all stay in their seats and sing "Sunshine on Leith" instead.'

In the days before and after the Scottish Cup final, some touching stories came to light.

Celtic striker but dyed-in-the-wool Hibee Leigh Griffiths was at the match (of course) and he spent some time at the next day's victory parade chatting to a terminally ill Hibs supporter, which was a nice thing to do.

Lifelong Hibs fan William Johnston died in hospital hours after the cup was won. His wife was able to let him know that Hibs had lifted the cup not long before he passed away.

Famous Hibee Derek Dick, better known as Fish, the lead singer of Marillion, lost his father in the days following the match.

Hugh Burns, father of Stevie and brother of Mike of the fanzine Mass Hibsteria, died four days before the final. Hugh had become a Hibs shareholder just a short time before his passing.

Hibs' first team coach John Doolan had lost his dad not long before the cup final. Mr Doolan's funeral was held at the beginning of the week before the final. John said, 'This club always gives you a lift and these fans always give you a lift. They've certainly given me that this weekend. Hibs are part of me forever after all of this. Once you understand this club, what it's all about and what the fans are like, it touches you big time.'

Mickey Weir, who was man of the Match when Hibs won the Skol Cup in 1991, was also thinking family thoughts. Mickey said, 'I am so glad that my sons could be there to see Hibs win the Scottish Cup because so many of my family members have passed away without witnessing it. I couldn't help but think about my granddad, my dad and my older uncles who never got to see that.

Alan Stubbs said that he told his players to change Hibs history not to be a part of a continuing story of Scottish Cup failure. All fourteen of them who were on the field certainly did that.

Driven on by the spirited and skilful John McGinn, inspired by an on-fire Anthony Stokes and led by an exemplary captain in David Gray, Conrad Logan, Darren McGregor, Paul Hanlon, Liam Fontaine, Lewis Stevenson, Fraser Fyvie, Dylan McGeouch, Jason Cummings, James Keatings, Liam Henderson and Niklas Gunnarsson, along with unused substitutes Mark Oxley, Chris Dagnall and Martin Boyle, wrote themselves into Hibernian history and by doing so made themselves true Hibernian legends. A banner held aloft in the Hibs end throughout the match had read 'TIME FOR HEROES'. Alan Stubbs' men recognised that time and became those heroes.

Interestingly, the last time Hibs won the Scottish Cup and no one needs reminding of when that was, they went on to win the League Championship in the 1902–03 season which followed their triumph. It would be nice to think that history might repeat itself in 2016–17.

Alan Stubbs will not be in charge of Hibs as they pursue promotion. Less than two weeks after writing himself into Hibs history forever, Stubbs chose to accept an offer to manage Rotherham United and bade his farewells to Easter Road. It did seem rather strange for a triumphant manager to leave a buoyant club, having just achieved Scottish Cup glory to join a team at the bottom of the English Championship with a stadium capacity of 12,000 and an underwhelming record of success but it has happened.

Alan Stubbs' record as Hibs manager makes for interesting reading. In seventy-two league matches, he had a win rate of 58%. His overall win rate in all competitive matches was also 58%. His longest unbeaten run was seventeen games from August to December 2015 and his longest winning streak was nine games between October and November 2015.

Stubbs' longest spell without victory was five games between February and March 2016. He had a good Edinburgh derby record winning two and drawing three out of six matches, and he was particularly successful in games against Premiership teams winning six and drawing four of eleven such matches. The only defeat was the unlucky loss to Ross County in the League Cup final.

Stubbs certainly knew how to play against Rangers as his record against the Light Blues – seven wins to six losses – clearly demonstrates. He was less successful against Falkirk, winning only two and losing four of eleven games with Peter Houston's side.

Stubbs record in the major cup competitions was exceptional as he reached the quarter-final and final of the League Cup and the semi-final and final of the Scottish Cup in his two seasons. The fact that the Scottish Cup final was won will ensure that Alan Stubbs will forever be enshrined in the annals of Hibernian history.

The Hibs support will, in the main, be very sorry to see Alan go. He had restored their pride in their team and delivered the Holy Grail. He moves to Yorkshire with the good wishes of the majority of those of a Hibernian persuasion ringing in his ears.

Since Bobby Atherton lifted Scottish football's most coveted trophy, quite a lot has happened. There have been two World Wars, the first aeroplane flight has taken place, five monarchs have ruled Britain, the world's population has more than trebled, man has set foot on the moon, there have been eleven Popes, eighteen US Presidents and twenty-one British Prime Ministers, twenty World Cups have taken place, eighteen teams have won the Scottish Cup, antibiotics have been discovered and television and computers have both been invented.

During those 114 long and painful years, Hibs supporters have had to reflect on the Proclaimers' most fitting lyrics, 'My heart was broken. My heart was broken. Sorrow, Sorrow, Sorrow'. Now, though, they can change their focus to later lines in that beautiful anthem and say, 'Thank you, thank you, thank you, thank you'.

When the Scottish Cup draw is made at the end of 2016, Hearts fans will be unable to sing, 'You last won the big cup in 1902.' Instead, Hibs supporters will sing 'We last won the big cup in 2016'. And that's a fact. We know, because when Hibs went up to lift the Scottish Cup, we were there.